Martin Kitchen has studied Modern Languages and Theology at the Universities of London and Manchester. He has exercised a varied ministry since ordination in the Church of England in 1979 and is now Vice-Dean of Durham Cathedral. His previous published works include *Ephesians (New Testament Readings)* (Routledge, 1994) and *Word of Truth* (1999), *Word in Our Time* (2000) and *Word Among Us* (2001) published by Canterbury Press.

A Talent for Living

Reflecting on Faith and Its Fruits

Martin Kitchen

First published in Great Britain in 2003 by
Society for Promoting Christian Knowledge
Holy Trinity Church
Marylebone Road
London NW1 4DU

British Library Cataloguing-in-Publication Data
A catalogue record for this book is available from the British Library

ISBN 0-281-05622-6

10 9 8 7 6 5 4 3 2

Designed and typeset by Kenneth Burnley, Wirral, Cheshire.
Printed in Great Britain by Bookmarque Ltd, Croydon, Surrey

Contents

With love and thanks
to the colleagues at Durham Cathedral
with whom I am and have been privileged to work
and to the clergy and people
of the Dioceses of Durham and Newcastle

Preface

I am very grateful to Ruth McCurry for the invitation to write this book; it has presented me with the challenge to put together a number of thoughts which I have been entertaining for some time about the relationship between the Bible and Christian discipleship. However, I must also thank her not only for sustained encouragement and support during the book's writing, but also for assistance and advice well above the call of duty in helping me to clarify the book's parameters.

As on many previous occasions I am grateful to my wife, Sheila, for taking time out of her own busy professional schedule to read through this text and make many helpful observations and suggestions. Her love and support remain as ever essential to all that I do.

Thanks are due also to the South London Church Fund and the Southwark Diocesan Board of Finance for permission to use material from 'O No, Not Ministry Again', published in *Kite*, Issue 11, July 1993; to the editor of *Affirming Catholicism* for permission to use material from 'Things Made of Clay', published in *Affirming Catholicism* 20, 1995; and to the executors of the estate of James MacGibbon for permission to quote from 'Not waving but drowning' by Stevie Smith. Hilaire Belloc's poem 'The false heart' is reprinted by permission of PFD on behalf of The Estate of Hilaire Belloc, copyright © 1970 The Estate of Hilaire Belloc.

The original impetus for an earlier form of this material came from invitations to address Retreats: for priests at Shepherd's Dene in September 2001 and for Self-Supporting Ministers at the same place in February 2002. Such invitations are typical of the generosity of spirit of the people of the north east of England. By way of a response, inadequate though it is, the book is dedicated with love and thanks to the colleagues with whom I am and have been privileged to work at Durham Cathedral and to the clergy and people of the Dioceses of Durham and Newcastle.

MARTIN KITCHEN

July 2003

1

Gifts and Talents

Reading

Matthew 25.14–30

'For it is as if a man, going on a journey, summoned his slaves and entrusted his property to them; to one he gave five talents, to another two, to another one, to each according to his ability. Then he went away. The one who had received the five talents went off at once and traded with them, and made five more talents. In the same way, the one who had the two talents made two more talents. But the one who had received the one talent went off and dug a hole in the ground and hid his master's money. After a long time the master of those slaves came and settled accounts with them. Then the one who had received the five talents came forward, bringing five more talents, saying, "Master, you handed over to me five talents; see, I have made five more talents." His master said to him, "Well done, good and trustworthy slave; you have been trustworthy in a few things, I will put you in charge of many things; enter into the joy of your master." And the one with the two talents also came forward, saying, "Master, you handed over to me two talents; see, I have made two more talents." His master said to him, "Well done, good and trustworthy slave; you have been trustworthy in a few things, I will put you in charge of many things; enter into the joy of your master." Then the one who had received the one talent also came forward, saying, "Master, I knew that you were a harsh man, reaping where you did not sow, and gathering where you did not scatter seed; so I was afraid, and I went and hid your talent in the ground. Here you have what is yours." But his master replied, "You wicked and lazy slave! You knew, did you, that I reap where I did not sow, and gather where I did not scatter? Then you ought to have invested my money with the bankers, and on my return I would have received what was my own with interest. So take the talent from him, and give it to the one with the ten talents. For to all those who have, more will be given, and they will have an abundance; but from those who have nothing, even what they have will be taken away. As for this worthless slave, throw him into the outer darkness, where there will be weeping and gnashing of teeth."'

Text

Romans 12.6

We have gifts that differ according to the grace given to us.

———•◆•———

This book addresses the question, 'What shall we do with what we have been given?' The question becomes even starker when we acknowledge that what we have been given includes both a particular life and a particular death. The parable of the talents, which is printed above, presents the issues in a clear and even stark fashion. It suggests that the question has to be faced in the context of ultimate judgement; it also invites us to understand it in the context of our relationships.

Maybe we do not like to think too much – or too literally – about judgement after death. So we might begin by suggesting that it is not so much our death as the death of Jesus that represents our final judgement. The people to whom Jesus spoke were able to take at face value his assertion that the kingdom of God was about to dawn. They had some idea of what it meant to say that God would come as King, for they knew their scriptures. The Psalms, which was their hymn book, along with other parts of the Old Testament, celebrated Jewish faith in the fact of God's kingship; and that meant that, as God's people, they would be delivered from those who oppressed them. It meant that they would be vindicated for all that they had suffered.

Jesus took all this a little further and said that the kingdom of God was about deliverance for all who suffer oppression of any kind, and it was about vindication and relief for all who are in pain. The kingdom also meant judgement for all the causes of that oppression, suffering and pain. One particular insight of Jesus was that this kingdom of God was imminent: it really was about to dawn. The early Christians soon came to realize that it was in the death and resurrection of Jesus that the kingdom of God was to be experienced, and it was supremely in the resurrection of Jesus that the earliest communities rejoiced. They were also able to remain firm in that faith in the face of fierce persecution.

Consequently, Christian belief is able to assert that judgement has already taken place. In the death of Jesus, all the evil in the world is judged, including our part in it; and in the case of human beings, it is forgiven. We might fear that we fall short of God's commandments; we might fear death; we might fear meeting with our maker; but evil has been overcome in the resurrection of Jesus from the dead, and forgiveness is available and free to all.

The question remains, however, 'What shall we do with what we have been given?'; for if judgement and forgiveness for our part in evil have already taken place in the past, so in the present our responsibility for the mutual well-being of all our sisters and brothers in the human race becomes a more urgent concern. We are all connected to each other, and we all suffer or rejoice together.

In the parable, the talent which was wasted by the wicked and lazy slave was not pocketed by the master; it was redistributed. We must be careful not to press the details of parables too closely, as though every little part necessarily carried its own particular meaning, but it is interesting to ask ourselves about the balances, the counterweights and the trade-offs which operate in the counting house of human behaviour.

Jesus told the parable of the talents as he was approaching his death. Indeed, it was as he approached his death that Jesus spoke more firmly than ever in terms of a judgement which God would carry out against the people of Israel for their rejection of Jesus. For Christian people, his death was not the end of him; rather, by raising him to life again, God said that the death of Jesus was the way to live. Failure to live in this way impacts upon those around us, even if it is only that, in the parable, it is those who have done well who benefit further from the wickedness and laziness of the 'unprofitable servant'.

There is a sense in which even our death is not lonely. It is the last journey we take, and nobody else can take it for us; but dying is something which everybody else without exception either has done or will do, and we are perhaps justified in claiming that we are never completely on our own as we undertake it. Indeed, the death of Jesus might, among other things, be taken to represent to us the degree to which we share with all our neighbours in the totality of human experience.

A talent in the Bible is a very large sum of money – about 15 years' wages. And the point about the judgement passed on the slaves here centres on what they did with what they had been given. As it turned out, the one who had been given the most made the most; the second one did well, too; but the third was judged wicked and lazy because he did nothing with what he had been given. He did not even have the initiative to put the money in the bank and let it earn a little interest.

Does it all seem very unfair? Well, the parable is about life, and whoever said that life should be fair? Perhaps that is a little too glib, but the question remains, 'What are you and I given?' And the answer? Life, for as long as it lasts; health, such as it is; gifts, such as they are. Wealth, maybe; certainly, for all of us in the West, a relatively high level of it. Power: all of us to some degree, as citizens, voters, church members. And what do we do with it?

Charles Wesley's hymn, 'A charge to keep I have', concludes with the chilling thought,

> Help me to watch and pray,
> and on thyself rely,
> assured, if I my trust betray,
> I shall forever die.

That is pretty strong stuff: 'if I my trust betray, I shall forever die'. But it underlines how important life is, and what great significance attaches to the business of getting our lives adjusted to the reality of God's kingdom.

Lent is a good time to ask ourselves the fundamental question, 'What shall we do with what we have been given?' The question is central to our 'final' judgement, and it impacts, whether or not we are aware of it, upon our neighbour.

We use the word 'talent' to mean ability, or capacity; Noel Coward had a 'talent to amuse', according to Sheridan Morley's 1969 biography. It would be good to think that the gifts of Christian people provided them with the capacity for living. Perhaps almost as famous as Noel Coward's talent is the saying of Jesus, 'I came that they may have life, and have it abundantly'. It would seem appropriate, therefore, that those who name him as Lord should show some signs of sharing his life and his zest for it – *abundantly*.

A talent, in the sense of a gift for living, requires the exercise of talents. Six such talents are discussed in this book, and it is reasonable to ask, 'Why these?' The answer is that each of them, in different ways, gets to the heart of what it is to be a Christian disciple. Some of them lie beneath the basic assumptions we have about ministry, and they have their roots in ordinary human experience; others relate directly to our understanding and use of the scriptures through which we hear the word of Christ, the good news of the reign of God, addressed to us as a human race. This book takes a look at some passages of the Bible which are associated with them and explores what meanings they might have in the context of the faith of the Christian.

The mention of gifts in Romans 12.6 has as its context the apostle's explanation of what it is to be 'justified by faith'. Earlier in the letter he has argued that the Jews have the Law to indicate what God requires of them, and that Gentiles have conscience for the same purpose. The problem is that neither Jew nor Gentile does what God requires in terms of social justice or personal righteousness; and the problem is solved by the coming of God into human affairs in the person of Jesus Christ. In Jesus, says Paul, God offers himself as the sacrifice between himself and humanity which brings about reconciliation. Full communion is therefore established in such a way that all people and nations are brought into renewed relationship with God, and they are capable of knowing this by believing in Jesus.

On this basis Paul urges his readers to offer themselves as a 'living sacrifice' – to match that which has already been offered by Jesus himself. The important point is that the metaphor of a 'living sacrifice' is a contradiction, for sacrificial animals die. But Paul is able to speak in this way partly because Jesus has already died, and partly because those readers, by sharing in the body of Jesus by baptism, have not only died with him, but have also been made to share in his resurrection. They are alive! Part of the offering of themselves consists in the exercise of the gifts which have been given to them by the grace of God, to be used for the mutual building up of all the believers.

This book takes up the theme of gifts, or talents. Each chapter takes a passage from the Bible along with another text and invites the readers, in the light of them, to reflect upon the talent under discussion as it may be observed in their own life and Christian service. Questions are provided as a means for developing further thoughts, and these may be helpful to both individuals and groups.

There are few things more irritating in friends and relatives than the experience of giving a gift and subsequently discovering that it has been abandoned or given away because it was not wanted. The gifts referred to here are talents, to be used in the business of living. Not everyone has been given them all – certainly not in the same degree – and yet there is something to be said for cultivating them, and even asking for them.

Certainly they need to be exercised, in the service not only of the Church, but also of the human race. We live in days when it is becoming increasingly clear that we must either unite or perish. Ancient animosities do not provide us with the tools for global social harmony, so we must learn to listen, to look and to serve our neighbour, to grow up in our relationships, to speak good news and to think clearly across the boundaries of race and religion, sex, gender and orientation, wealth and poverty, social class and caste. Ordinary Christian people must do this and so provide an example for those in positions of leadership to follow.

These issues go to the heart of what it is to be human; as such they impinge on the ultimate questions of life and death. Hence the question, 'What shall we do with the talents we have been given?', and our consideration of its implications for life, death, judgement and relationships.

2

Looking

Reading

2 Corinthians 4.1–12

Therefore, since it is by God's mercy that we are engaged in this ministry, we do not lose heart. We have renounced the shameful things that one hides; we refuse to practise cunning or to falsify God's word; but by the open statement of the truth we commend ourselves to the conscience of everyone in the sight of God. And even if our gospel is veiled, it is veiled to those who are perishing. In their case the god of this world has blinded the minds of the unbelievers, to keep them from seeing the light of the gospel of the glory of Christ, who is the image of God. For we do not proclaim ourselves; we proclaim Jesus Christ as Lord and ourselves as your slaves for Jesus' sake. For it is the God who said, 'Let light shine out of darkness,' who has shone in our hearts to give the light of the knowledge of the glory of God in the face of Jesus Christ.

But we have this treasure in [things made of] clay, so that it may be made clear that this extraordinary power belongs to God and does not come from us. We are afflicted in every way, but not crushed; perplexed, but not driven to despair; persecuted, but not forsaken; struck down, but not destroyed; always carrying in the body the death of Jesus, so that the life of Jesus may also be made visible in our bodies. For while we live, we are always being given up to death for Jesus' sake, so that the life of Jesus may be made visible in our mortal flesh. So death is at work in us, but life in you.

Text

Mark 9.2–3

Six days later, Jesus took with him Peter and James and John, and led them up a high mountain apart, by themselves. And he was transfigured before them, and his clothes became dazzling white, such as no one on earth could bleach them.

———•◆•———

The way light enters the body through the eye is a marvellous process. It comes in through the pupil, and its rays are focused in such a way that an image is produced on the retina. The millions of cells which make up the retina convert the image into a pattern of nerve impulses which are transmitted along the optic nerve to the brain. The brain processes this information to produce a single, co-ordinated image. This is what enables us to see; it is therefore also the background to the metaphor of looking, which is central to Christian experience and thinking.

Looking is not a passive experience; it is an action by which we engage with the world in which our Christian life is worked out. For Christian people the skill of looking is not just a question of letting our eyes do the work for which they are intended. God, we are told, *saw* that the creation was 'very good' (Genesis 1.31); prophets *saw* what they were to say (see Isaiah 6.1 and, especially, Amos 1.1: 'The words of Amos, . . . which he saw . . .'); there are stories in the Gospels which tell of Jesus enabling people to *see* (Mark, Matthew, Luke, John); '*seeing*' the risen Jesus was important to the early Christians for the conviction that he had been raised to life after his crucifixion (see

Matthew 28.17; Luke 24.11, 31, 34; and count the number of times that the word 'see' occurs in John 20); and St Paul bases his call to apostleship on his having 'seen the Lord' (see Galatians 1.16; 1 Corinthians 9.1). These references all suggest that there is something more at stake here than physical seeing; and these come together in the story of the transfiguration in Mark and its parallels in Matthew and Luke. We are called to see not just the ordinary things of life, wonderful as they are; we are called to see the treasure of God which all those things may be carrying.

Nothing much of any consequence happens in a group – or in the life of an individual – without vision. Indeed, Proverbs 29.18 says that where there is no vision, people perish. Wisdom lies in both taking an overall view and paying attention to the detail of what is going on. A professional lay trainer with whom I once worked used to talk about 'helicoptering': zooming out to get the context right and to get a general view of all that was going on, while also zooming in to become familiar with the details and the intimacies of things.

All of us in our Christian lives are involved in 'overseeing', or 'looking over', the world, our society and the community in which we exercise some responsibility, *in the light of the gospel*. That is what looking is about: how is the good news of Jesus faring here? Indeed, where is Jesus Christ here? How might he be named as incarnate among these human realities?

Vision is what St Paul is talking about in 2 Corinthians 4, both the necessity of looking and the reality of the thing seen. 'We have this treasure in things made of clay', he says, and there are two points to be made about this text: the first has to do with 'this treasure', and second with 'things made of clay'.

There are two aspects to Paul's vision: first, 'this treasure' is the vision which is crucial to apostolic ministry. The vision was crucial for Paul, for it is clear from the context of this verse that 'this treasure' is the same as 'this ministry', to which the apostle refers in 2 Corinthians 4.1: 'Therefore, since it is by God's mercy that we are engaged in this ministry . . .' Earlier in the Epistle,

Paul has given thanks that God led him from Troas, in Asia, to Corinth, in Macedonia; from Asia to Europe. 'Thanks be to God', he says, 'who always leads us in triumph, and through us spreads the fragrance of the knowledge of him everywhere.'

He likens his progress as an apostle who goes about preaching the gospel to the kind of parade that would be held for a general to celebrate a military triumph. These were great occasions, when the victor after a battle was paraded through the streets of Rome, and everyone sang his praises. Paul's reflection on such a glorious spectacle leads him eventually to consider the glory in the face of Moses as he talked with God. The scriptures tell us that this was so bright when he came down from Mount Sinai that a veil had to be placed over his head so that he did not dazzle the Israelites.

Paul draws a contrast with Moses wearing his veil, and says, 'We all' – that is, all of us engaged in 'this ministry' – we all 'with unveiled face, beholding the glory of the Lord, are being changed into his likeness, from one degree of glory to another.' This vision – of the change that he and his colleagues undergo as they undertake the apostolic mission and thereby see the face of Christ – is what keeps Paul going, encouraging him in his ministry. He cannot possibly lose heart, for he has received this ministry by the mercy of God; neither will he use dirty or underhand means to advance the gospel. And the transformation which he experiences is a foretaste of the light of eternal glory. 'We have this treasure in things made of clay', he says; and 'this treasure' is the vision which is crucial to his apostolic task.

But also, this vision is crucial to apostolic ministry for us. In our day, centuries after Paul, there is more to be said about that vision. For by acknowledging the glory which goes along with proclaiming the good news, the apostle paved the way for the later development of the belief that all humankind is called to participate in the life of God, which is to be seen in the face of Jesus Christ.

That is why I want to refer to St Mark's Gospel (Matthew and Luke take up Mark's story, expand and adapt it). In Mark 9 there is the story of Jesus being transfigured in the presence of the disciples, and the same tradition about Moses on the mountaintop lies behind that. This story is central to Mark, who provides no resurrection appearances at the end of his Gospel. The story of the glory of Jesus which he tells is of a glory which is right in the middle of life. Jesus takes three disciples up a mountain and is 'transfigured' in front of them. The pace with which the story is told suggests that this happens as he leads them; they see his back, and so it is his clothing which shines. To note that is to see why there is no mention of Jesus' face in Mark: the disciples cannot see it. What they see is an anticipation of the glory of the world to come, in which the righteous shine with white robes.

This all takes place 'six days' after Jesus had promised the disciples that there were some standing there with him who would not see death until they saw the kingdom of God come in power. This was after he had asked them who he was, and after Peter had confessed, 'You are the Messiah.' Jesus had commanded them not to tell anyone about him, and had forewarned them of his death and resurrection, concluding with that promise.

As far as Mark is concerned, then, this is the fulfilment of that promise. The Second Letter of Peter later makes the connection between that story and the 'divine power' by which we are all enabled to become 'partakers of the divine nature'. Later theologians observed that this purpose of God is central to the mystery of the incarnation. 'He became human that we might become divine', in the words of St Athanasius; or 'the human being is an animal who has received the vocation to become God', as St Basil of Caesarea said. This is the calling addressed to the human race; this is the invitation which comes to all men and women in Christ. For us, it is not just an encouraging and sustaining vision which keeps apostolic ministry going; it is the foundation for it, the whole motivation for it and, indeed, all the content of it. This is the destiny of us all, of the whole of humankind, 'to share in the life of God'.

But we have this treasure in things made of clay. There is a fascinating story told concerning the moving in 1163 of the relics of Edward the Confessor, who founded Westminster Abbey in 1065. Pope Alexander III had canonized Edward in February 1161, and at the ceremony of his translation Aelred, Abbot of Rievaulx, preached the sermon on the text which was normally used on such occasions: 'No one after lighting a lamp puts it under the bushel . . .' (Matthew 5.15), and the remains of Edward were removed from a tomb in front of the high altar to be set up in a shrine, as if on a candlestick, that it might give light to all that were in the house.

The problem was that it didn't. The light was there, raised on a candlestick, but there was no response to it. Not even the celebrated piety of Edward the Confessor could enlighten the atmosphere of that gloomy occasion. The president at the ceremony was Thomas Becket, the Archbishop of Canterbury. His days of carousing with King Henry II were long past (they were colourfully represented, some readers may remember, in a film in the mid-1960s, *Becket*, which starred Richard Burton and Peter O'Toole), and the famous feud between King and Archbishop was just getting under way. Imagine: Henry, delighted at getting a royal predecessor canonized, with all the clout this will inevitably give him in his argument with the Church; and Thomas, quietly confident that the canonization of Anselm, a former Archbishop of Canterbury, which he had proposed to Pope Alexander just a few months before, will work in *his* favour.

Now there's a network of dynamics to match a church council meeting! And this occasion did not just prompt murderous thoughts: it ended in murder, 'in the cathedral', too. It stands, of course, for the whole, sad, human condition. There was envy, manipulation – and we all know how religion can always help here – and lust for power. We can probably all think of illustrations closer to home and on the international political scene; yes, there is 'treasure' in a vision of humanity sharing in the life of God, but *we have this treasure in things made of clay.*

This brings me to the other thing to be said about this passage: this image, of things made of clay, is not primarily of containment, but of change, of transfiguration. Certainly the pots contain the treasure: there are examples enough in ancient Greek and Latin literature of earthenware money-boxes, of jars for holding treasure, especially in victory processions, and so on. But the more important point is the fact that the containers, the pots, are changed by what they carry. This is clear from three points which are present in the text: first, the context is of the face of Moses, which was transformed and shining as he bore the tables of the Law; second, Paul speaks of manifesting in his body *at the same time* both the death and the life of the resurrected Jesus; and finally, the word 'vessel' is a word used for all sorts of things in Greek: vessels for cooking, utensils, implements, tools, gear, things; chattels in a victory procession; someone has even suggested that the primary reference of this metaphor might be to the individual letters of the Hebrew alphabet, which Paul is at pains to place in an order of importance secondary to that of Christ. So: pots, paraphernalia, persons or pigment – all are possible. 'We have this treasure in things made of clay.' St Paul is talking about vessels which *become* treasure.

'Things made of clay' are, of course, always liable to return to the dust from which they took their origin. People decline: their bones grow brittle, their limbs weaken, their hearing fails, and their eyes go blind. Pots are broken: sometimes to be mended, sometimes to be thrown away. Tools go rusty. Ink and letters fade. Apostles – and Christian people, clergy and lay – suffer affliction, perplexity and persecution. Bodies die! 'While we live, we are always being given up to death for Jesus' sake.' Paul is talking, not primarily about containment, but rather about transfiguration. The image is of the face of Moses shot through with glory; it is of the words of scripture, which *are* dead, and which *make for* death, as far as Paul is concerned, without the Spirit who gives life; the image is of the apostle himself who will not be crushed, nor driven to despair, nor destroyed. The 'earthen vessels', the things made of clay, are themselves changed into treasure. Mud is made into amethyst; dust into diamonds.

Some friends of mine once attended a conference, in the course of which they visited a ceramics factory. 'There', said their host, 'is a pile of plates; and there is some paint. What I want to invite you to do is to paint your plate, and then decide whether you want to break it – and how. After you have broken it, you may decide how you want it put together again; the English way, or the Chinese way. The English way is to make an invisible join and paint and glaze over it so that nobody knows it has been broken. The Chinese way is to start by edging all the pieces in gold. Why is it edged in gold? Because *this plate has a history*.'

We Christian people are, and we deal with, plates that have a history; 'We have this treasure in things made of clay.' We might well want to ask what all this has to do with the exercise of Christian discipleship, especially insofar as it involves 'looking over' what lies before us with a view to seeing how the gospel is faring. It seems to me that it has to do with a transfiguring vision. It is about enabling all the people among whom we live and work to see the treasure of God's love made real within our human culture and our shared experience, and to see the very clay of their existence transfigured by the Spirit of Christ.

Now that is some task! For underlying it is always the possibility that it will crucify – (that is one of the meanings of the word, 'crucial'); 'while we live, we are always being given up to death for Jesus' sake'. Neither is it just the big issues that are the killers, like the way you try to make a difference to the parish, or sphere of work – whatever it may be – in its presentation of the gospel. It's not just about the great schemes with church schools and the local council and the member of parliament and the church council – or even the General Synod, if you are on it – and all that. It is the daily being put to death by the constant demands that life makes upon us, along with, on top of all that, the challenge of making some sense of it all as Christian disciples; and we must not forget that, sometimes, it is other Christian disciples who make our pilgrimage difficult. All those plates, and all that history – and all the expense on the gold of forgiveness! *All* of it has to be offered, in the task of enabling human beings to acknowledge their participation in God.

'Who is sufficient for these things?' (2 Corinthians 2.16). St Paul answered his own question: 'Our sufficiency is from God'; and later on, in a different context, he is told, 'My grace is sufficient for you, for power is made perfect in weakness' (2 Corinthians 12.9). There are times when we might be able to contain neither the trauma nor the treasure of what happens to us; but, by the mercy of God, we will be transfigured – 'from glory into glory'. Our constant prayer has to be for a good stiff draught of the Holy Spirit for each other, that we may find this sufficiency sufficient.

There is a sense in which visions are granted rather than worked up. Jesus in Mark 9 *takes* the disciples up the mountain without their asking him to do so. On the other hand, Paul *invites* the Corinthians to look at things from his perspective. These two aspects of looking belong together: what is required is a certain alertness, a readiness to look for the illuminating presence of Christ in all that we see. The key to seeing would appear to be thanksgiving (2 Corinthians 2.14). In Paul giving thanks is the opening chord of most of his letters. He thanks God for his ministry, for his friends, for God's protection and for his new life in Christ.

The Letter to the Ephesians urges its readers, 'Sleeper, awake! Rise from the dead, and Christ will shine on you.' This looks like a quotation from a hymn, which may or may not have been known to the readers; the writer is urging the readers to get out of bed, rub their eyes, see what is going on around them and live their lives in the light of Christ.

The alternative is dangerous. The story of the transfiguration in Mark concludes with the three disciples descending the mountain with Jesus and finding the remaining disciples failing to cast out a dumb spirit from a boy. While up the mountain the three of them had been unable to respond adequately to what they saw; now they come down and see that the outcome of their experience has to do with overcoming whatever it is that prevents people from hearing and speaking.

Visions have to be translated into reality. The call of Isaiah was by something which he saw (Isaiah 6.1ff.), and Amos 1.1 speaks of 'the words . . . which he saw'. Having seen what it was they had to do, they were called to put it into practice. Similarly, the task of Christian disciples today is not just to enjoy seeing things: it is to look and take in how things are, then to imagine ways in which an even broader vision for the kingdom of God might be brought to realization, and then to get on and bring it about. And that will take some thinking about.

Vision has to be the basis of our action, and we hold on to that by keeping the possibility of transfiguration always before us – like Moses who, as Hebrews 11.27 might be translated, 'persevered as though the unseen one were constantly before his eyes'. It also has to inform the way in which we put into practice whatever vision we develop. As it was for Peter, James and John, our vision will be shared with other people: some of them will be fellow disciples, some of them will be our neighbours outside the churches.

As human beings we are given eyes and the gift of sight so that we may find food and shelter, share our life with our neighbours and enjoy our world. For Christian people sight is also the means by which our spirits may be nourished as we see what effect the coming of the kingdom of God might have on our communities, our relationships and our lives. That vision is not just of the way things are; it is also for the way things could be once the clay jars of our lives have experienced the grace of transfiguration.

———•◆•———

Questions

- What are the things in our personal history, or those of our family or community, which have broken us?
- Can we see the cracks, or do we keep them hidden?
- In what areas of our discipleship and our life together do we need a new vision?
- What are the daily things of which we cannot see the point?
- With whom will we attempt to develop that vision?
- How will we go about seeing it?
- What steps might we take to put its implications into practice?

3

Listening

Reading

1 Samuel 3

Now the boy Samuel was ministering to the LORD under Eli. The word of the LORD was rare in those days; visions were not widespread.

At that time Eli, whose eyesight had begun to grow dim so that he could not see, was lying down in his room; the lamp of God had not yet gone out, and Samuel was lying down in the temple of the LORD, where the ark of God was. Then the LORD called, 'Samuel! Samuel!' and he said, 'Here I am!' and ran to Eli, and said, 'Here I am, for you called me.' But he said, 'I did not call; lie down again.' So he went and lay down. The LORD called again, 'Samuel!' Samuel got up and went to Eli, and said, 'Here I am, for you called me.' But he said, 'I did not call, my son; lie down again.' Now Samuel did not yet know the LORD, and the word of the LORD had not yet been revealed to him. The LORD called Samuel again, a third time. And he got up and went to Eli, and said, 'Here I am, for you called me.' Then Eli perceived that the LORD was calling the boy. Therefore Eli said to Samuel, 'Go, lie down; and if he calls you, you shall say, "Speak, LORD, for your servant is listening."' So Samuel went and lay down in his place.

Now the LORD came and stood there, calling as before, 'Samuel! Samuel!' And Samuel said, 'Speak, for your servant is listening.'

Then the LORD said to Samuel, 'See, I am about to do something in Israel that will make both ears of anyone who hears of it tingle. On that day I will fulfil against Eli all that I have spoken concerning his house, from beginning to end. For I have told him that I am about to punish his house for ever, for the iniquity that he knew, because his sons were blaspheming God, and he did not restrain them. Therefore I swear to the house of Eli that the iniquity of Eli's house shall not be expiated by sacrifice or offering for ever.'

Samuel lay there until morning; then he opened the doors of the house of the LORD. Samuel was afraid to tell the vision to Eli. But Eli called Samuel and said, 'Samuel, my son.' He said, 'Here I am.' Eli said, 'What was it that he told you? Do not hide it from me. May God do so to you and more also, if you hide anything from me of all that he told you.' So Samuel told him everything and hid nothing from him. Then he said, 'It is the LORD; let him do what seems good to him.'

As Samuel grew up, the LORD was with him and let none of his words fall to the ground. And all Israel from Dan to Beer-sheba knew that Samuel was a trustworthy prophet of the LORD. The LORD continued to appear at Shiloh, for the LORD revealed himself to Samuel at Shiloh by the word of the LORD.

Text
Luke 24.19

'What things?'

————•◆•————

Samuel is one of the most remarkable characters in the Old Testament. We frequently refer to him as 'the prophet Samuel', but he is more than a prophet. In the first place, he is the successor to Eli, the last of the judges. Second, he is associated closely with the priesthood by virtue of his residence at Shiloh with Eli and in his assuming the priestly functions of Eli as Eli becomes old and blind and falls from favour with God. Samuel is also the means by which the monarchy is established; he selects and anoints both Saul, first king, and David, his successor.

There are two reasons why I turn to 1 Samuel 3 and to the call of this man when he was still a boy. First, it is because Samuel is such a significant character in the history of Israel; second, it is because this passage is one of the most beautiful narratives in scripture. I used to recite it at the start of Salvation Army Sunday School, when I was a boy; the same passage would be recited each Sunday morning for three months, so it was easy to learn parts of the Bible by heart. I can also remember a hymn we used to sing:

> Hushed was the evening hymn;
> The temple courts were dark;
> The lamp was burning dim
> Before the sacred ark,
> When suddenly, a voice divine
> Rang through the silence of the shrine.

The twilight in which the story begins is a metaphor for the moral and spiritual twilight of the nation. 'Visions were not widespread', we are told. There is only the faintest glimmer of light at the end of the day; Eli the priest is blind, and his blindness is more than physical, for it mirrors the lack of prophetic vision in the nation. The only hope focuses upon about-to-be-enlightened Samuel. Back in Genesis 3 God had come looking for Adam 'at the time of the evening breeze'; now he comes to his own house looking for Samuel.

The threefold repetition of God's calling of Samuel awakens our expectancy as, with the moral support of old Eli (who for all his faults remains wise and courageous), Samuel responds to the voice of God. 'Speak, LORD, for your servant is ready to hear', he says, and thus begins a lifetime's conversation with the Almighty. Samuel learns to listen, and Israel's fortunes take a turn for the better. The story plays a part in the nation's saving narrative, for here is a prophet who will see the word and hear the vision.

With what foreboding does the young Samuel wait for the dawn? The German poet, Eduard Mörike, has a poem entitled 'Ein Stündlein wohl vor Tag', 'An hour before the dawn', in which the poet lies half asleep just before daybreak and hears a bird singing in a nearby tree of the infidelity of his or her lover. The poem concludes:

> O no! please say no more!
> Silence! I will not hear!
> Fly off, fly off, get out of my tree;
> O love and loyalty are a dream
> an hour before the dawn!

Samuel also faces a faithless morning, but one which, for all its horror, still bears the ambiguity of promise. What Samuel heard as the night began was God's reaction to what the reader is told in chapter 2, and it is enough to make the ears tingle. It is a story of infidelity and of the withdrawal of God's forgiveness from Eli's house. So the events unfold: the ark of the covenant is captured; Hophni and Phinehas, Eli's sons, are killed; Eli hears the news and falls down dead; and Phinehas's wife, expecting a child, goes into labour. It seems strange that someone attending the birth should say at this point, 'Don't panic!' (It is almost reminiscent of the character of Corporal Jones in the television series, *Dad's Army*.) The woman, who is unnamed, fails to respond, and the child taken from her womb is called Ichabod – *the glory is departed*!

According to 1 Samuel 2.25, it is all due to a failure to *listen*: 'But they would not listen to the voice of their father; for it was the will of the LORD to kill them.' Eli failed to listen, and his sons failed to listen. Samuel, the son of Hannah and Elkanah, whose birth was thanks to God's having listened to his mother's prayer (cf. 1 Samuel 1), did listen, and the gift of listening marked his life.

Another great listener was Jesus on the road to Emmaus. His great question, 'What things?', is addressed to two disciples on the day on which Jesus' tomb has been found empty. The two of them are talking about what they have heard of the events at the tomb, and he draws level with them to join in the conversation. The striking thing about the structure of the story is that what he hears them talking about concerns what has been happening to himself, and yet he asks them to tell it to him in their own words.

His asking them the question, 'What things?', when those *things* concern him, is a case of textbook counselling; it also provides, incidentally, a fascinating insight into the nature of the Passion and the resurrection. The events of the day are all about Jesus, of course; but his concern is that the two disciples should tell the story as their own. This enables them to express their response, which at this stage is their sorrow and their horror. For Cleopas and his companion the death of Jesus represents the dashing of their hopes, confounded by the disgraceful behaviour of their own religious leaders. The stories of the empty tomb simply add to their sense of confusion. However, it also indicates how the story of Jesus is the story of all who will engage with his story; for it is on that basis that Jesus is able to take them on to further understanding of *the things about himself*; for such things are also about *themselves*.

According to Thomas Hart in *The Art of Christian Listening* (The Paulist Press, NJ, 1980: 9), listening is sacramental. It may take time; it may be exacting; it may be tedious; and the people we have to listen to may be ugly or unpleasant; but listening is fundamental to being a Christian.

The Church spends a lot of its time talking. The 'Decade of Evangelism' in the 1990s was widely perceived as an opportunity to *tell* people what we wanted them to know; and the current passion in the Church for advertisements and logos can give the impression not so much of confidence as of a loss of nerve. This is not to say that the Church has nothing to proclaim (see later, Chapter 6); rather that we might convey more 'good news' if we were to spend more time listening – like both Samuel and Jesus.

The things we need to listen to are several: our neighbours, our culture, ourselves – and God in all of them. When we spend time, energy and concentration on *listening* to someone, we convey to them that they are worth listening to, that what they have to say is significant, and that therefore they themselves are significant to us.

To take first the example of Jesus, we need to listen first to our neighbours, to *people*. One aspect of this is focus; we have all probably met people who had the capacity to make us feel that, for the five minutes that we were with them, we were the only person whose concerns mattered. And we probably all remember having conversations during which we have looked over the shoulder of the person with whom we have been speaking, in order to look out for someone more interesting, more important.

Another aspect is unconditionality. Those who are trained in coaching and counselling learn to listen to the other person in such a way that they may say whatever they like, and the listener does not pass judgement. Such unconditionality may create problems when we are told confidences – such as when priests hear confession; or when what we are told may lead to conflicts of obligations and loyalties. We have to learn to live with those; Dietrich Bonhoeffer spoke about 'the luxury of a clear conscience', and that is something that is not always possible to the person who takes seriously the call to listen to another person.

A third aspect is silence. As Hart points out (pp. 22–4), we are not responsible for our neighbour's life; we are not there to remove their problems or their pain, nor to offer greater experience, nor to make them a different person. The listening itself is what is important, and we need to keep quiet in order to do it.

It was on the basis of his listening to the two disciples that Jesus was able to refer them to a wider context of understanding: the scriptures, with which they are familiar, and the life of the man they have loved, whom Jesus treats – though they are talking about him – as though he were a third party.

Second, however, to follow the example of Samuel, we must listen to *our culture*. And that culture is very mixed indeed, with good and evil. What Samuel had to hear concerned God's sentence upon the nation and upon Eli and his family, who should have exercised a more responsible leadership.

Two aspects (among others) of our culture – power and money – have recently been addressed by the Church of England's Doctrine Commission in its 2003 report, *Being Human*. In the case of power, we might note that we pride ourselves on living in a democracy, and yet, at the time of writing, the British government has been involved in a war against Iraq upon the basis that the regime we were attacking was a threat to our security because of its possession of chemical, biological and nuclear 'weapons of mass destruction'. The validity of the case has now been questioned. We were also assured that, for all that there was no sanction by the United Nations for the war, that organization would be involved in the revitalizing of the country after the conflict. This has not happened, but the United States and the United Kingdom have been allowed a mandate effectively to control between them the country and its economy.

One of the questions posed by this state of affairs is that of the accountability of elected rulers, not just to the majority views of the people who elect them – which is an issue in itself – but to some agreed standards of morality, justice and truth-telling. The Doctrine Commission report suggests that people often have more power than they are aware of; we might ask ourselves, in what ways might democratic power be expressed and exercised on occasions when elected governments act in this way?

Related to the issue of power is that of money. Terry Eagleton compiles a list of global ills in *Sweet Violence* (Blackwell Publishing, Oxford, 2003: 295) which includes deepening poverty, widening inequality, enforced migration, ethnic warfare, social devastation, natural pillage and military aggression. In the light of these there is no place for moral complacency. Many of these are the result of Western policies towards the rest of the world and therefore are directly related to the question of power which has just been raised.

The Doctrine Commission report draws attention to the issue of money itself, rather than the broader question of wealth, and notes how a market in currency has developed over recent years, with laws of its own which frequently govern the foreign policies of the West. Many readers of this book will wish to style them-selves 'democratic'. We need to listen to those sounds in our culture of an economic system which allows its priorities to be determined largely by the desires of transnational companies to make profits, at whatever the cost to local communities which are the producers of the goods we like to buy so cheaply.

On the other hand, there is much in our culture to which we might listen with profit; and the two voices have to be heard together. We live in an age which has been described as 'post-modern'. There are those who try to shrug the phenomenon off by feigning ignorance of what the term means, but it is worth a look.

There is a nostalgia prevalent in our culture which attempts to hark back to a supposed better age. About 30 years ago a book was published by Geoffrey Wilson entitled *Hooligan: A History of Respectable Fears*. Wilson had undertaken research in newspapers going back to the 1830s and noted that there was a tendency to assert that life had been much better and safer 20 years before, while 40 years ago English society had been nigh-on perfect. Such nostalgia frequently masquerades as 'tradition' in the Church, and is to be seen, for example, in the passion with which we collude with those conservative forces which seek to defend the unchanging inviolability of our church buildings and prevent appropriate development of them for contemporary uses. Another is the antiquarianism which dominates the study of liturgy; it has provided certainly the Church of England with several volumes of minutely researched orders of service, the authènticity of which, we are assured, goes back centuries. The results of all this work, however, offer little by way of engagement with the contemporary needs of those who want to pray, whether alone or together, and force them instead to manage large volumes of material which is authoritarian, long-winded and pernickety.

We live in challenging times; and, as I have said, one label which attaches to them is 'postmodern'. Postmodernity gets its name by distinction from 'modernity', which, in its turn, was the contrast to 'antiquity'. (This is something of an over-simplification, but it is not too wide of the mark.) According to Jonathan Israel (*Radical Enlightenment*, Oxford, 2000: 6) what characterized antiquity was a number of features of political and social arrangements which could be systematized as: monarchy, aristocracy, ecclesiastical power, unaccountability, the authority of tradition and economic stagnation. Israel points out that modernity, which was born with the Enlightenment, made a number of demands: that knowledge should be derived from evidence; that truth should be derived from evidence and reasoning; that government should be by the consent of the governed; that people should have the right to question unexamined assumptions regarding knowledge, truth and government. From these desires developed the modern world with, among other things, its concern for human rights and scientific enquiry.

Postmodernity draws attention to the problems posed by the very freedoms which modernity sought: that evidence can be ambiguous, that it can be rigged, and that it does not lead to certainty; that reason can be used selectively and understood narrowly to exclude what is considered undesirable by the ruling group; that democracies, so called, can be imperialistic; and that economics is not necessarily democratic, and large international companies are wealthier than many national economies, but not subject to democratic scrutiny.

In addition, movements have arisen which draw attention to the absence or the abuse of reason: feminism, the movement for the recognition of the equality between women and men, has also raised the whole range of issues concerning sex and sexual orientation; post-colonialism and multiculturalism have drawn attention to the fact that ways of thinking about cultures different from the white and the Western, combined with particular policies of some Western governments, have exercised an inordinate level of control over the lives of people perceived to be too 'different' from the determining identity of those with power, one aspect of this being overt racism. Religious movements also are now recognized as having an inevitable cultural foundation.

Certainly the whole philosophical edifice which dates back to Thomas Aquinas, and upon which Christianity has relied, has been subject to radical questioning and now virtual abandonment, and Western society has become practically atheistic – at least in the traditional sense. However, it is quite clear that 'spirituality' is far from dead; and the growth of learning in the twentieth century paid great attention to language and textuality.

In the area of spirituality, all kinds of people in our society are engaged in exploration. Not long ago I attended a meeting which concluded with lunch. I had eaten rather hurriedly and had just said to a colleague, 'You must excuse me; I have to get away to another meeting', when she said, 'I used to take Lent very seriously when I was young.'

Sensing that the conversation might be more important than the meeting, I was conscious of switching deliberately into my best 'non-directive' behaviour and said, 'You used to take Lent seriously?'

'Yes; I was brought up a Catholic, and we would make a big thing of it at school. I gave up Mars bars, collected money for missions and was really committed. But when I reached the age of 19 I realized I no longer believed it all, so gave it all up.'

'You realized you no longer believed it all, so gave it all up?'

'Yes; but I still pray.'

'You still pray?'

'What do you think of that?'

'I think the question is, what do *you* think of it? What happens when you pray?'

She thought for a moment and then said, 'I think that a part of me speaks to a deeper part of me. What do you make of that?'

I told her: 'Well, as I say, what is more significant is what *you* make of it; but if I might make one observation, it occurs to me that it might be important to keep the conversation going.'

'Thank you; I will. Now I must let you get to your meeting.'

There are spiritualities abroad in our culture which we do well to encourage; they may be manifestations of the Spirit of God.

Modern interest in language started with the work of Ferdinand de Saussure. His *Course in General Linguistics* was not published in his lifetime (he died in 1913), but was put together from the notebooks of his students and brought out in 1916. Saussure broke with tradition in the study of languages by moving away from descriptions dictated by the forms used to describe the classical languages. He was concerned to study language as it was currently spoken and therefore drew a distinction between tracing the historical development of language through time, which he labelled the 'diachronic' approach, and paying attention to how it functioned at the present moment, which he called 'synchronic'.

Next, he noted that the meaning borne by a linguistic sign – be it sound, word, sentence or longer example of language – was arbitrary. That is to say, there is no essential or necessary connection between the sign and the thing signified, so meaning is shared and discovered by means of conventions agreed between the speakers of a language.

Third, he saw that linguistic signs operated by a system of difference. A simple example of this is the way we know – in language – that a *bat* is not the same as a *cat*: because the sound represented by the letter 'b' is different from that represented by 'c'. This is particularly interesting in cases where the different sounds are made in the same part of the mouth, but with difference only in, say, the vibration of the vocal chords, which is known as voicing, or in the strength with which breath is expelled, which is known as aspiration, represented in English at the beginning of words with the letter 'h'. The two features come close together in the differences between words such as *bat* and *pat*.

Finally, Saussure noted that the speaker of language plays a part in the language system different from that which had previously been understood. If language is a system of signs, then the focus of language is not so much the speaker, who is simply a participant in it, but rather language itself; language comes to expression through the speaker, and the speaker is a function of language, rather than the other way round.

Broadly speaking, these features of Saussure's work together comprise what is known as 'structuralism'. Naturally, since his day Saussure's insights have been taken further and developed by others. The importance of them for Christians lies in the ways in which we might apply them to our reading of the scriptures. This brings us to consider another aspect of listening, which is to *the Bible*.

It has often been said that Christianity, along with Judaism and Islam, are 'religions of the book'. They have in common the Hebrew scriptures, and while Muslims add to these their Koran, Christians have their New Testament, which title draws attention to the antiquity of the 'Old'.

The nature of contemporary thinking about language and texts means that we have much both to learn and to say within current debates. There is a tradition that writing is inferior to speech, which is, in turn, inferior to thought. Recent discussions have queried this tradition and asserted that writing has a significance of its own (and there is more on this in Chapter 6). Professor Christopher Evans has suggested that the writing of the Gospels themselves might have signalled a 'lack of nerve' on the part of the early Church. However, in the light of research into the nature of writing and texts, one wonders whether, on the contrary, there is something about writing which is a mark of confidence in the text, in oneself and in the community. With increasing interest in the fact and language of writing and texts, which amounts almost to a philosophy of writing, we have things to learn and to contribute.

The Bible stands at the fountain-head of Christian tradition. Not all Christians are able to make the same doctrinal affirmations about it that many do, but they may well wish still to talk in terms of its 'inspiration', for, in some way, God undoubtedly breathes through its pages. Part of the problem lies in the fact that the doctrine of inspiration was first elaborated in the context of the European Reformation, when it was important for the Reformers to establish an absolute authority for the Bible over against that of the Roman Catholic Church. The doctrine became further nuanced in the light of those approaches to the text of the Bible which arose as a result of the Enlightenment, when scholars began to explore both the historical reliability of the scriptures in the light of their own inconsistencies and the nature of its literary make-up and internal textual interdependence.

It is not easy to say how a contemporary doctrine of inspiration – if such is desirable! – might be developed which would take seriously not only the approaches of historical and literary criticism but also the insights of textuality and the vagaries of meaning. Such a doctrine would also need to recognize the difficulty noted by recent scholars (such as David Parker and Bart Ehrmann) of determining precisely how to reconstruct the best biblical text from the many examples of it which are in existence. David Law has attempted to elaborate such a doctrine, with the use of a concept of 'ciphers', derived from the work of Karl Jaspers. He suggests that religious texts consist of signs and symbols which go beyond ordinary human experience and both embody and convey the transcendent.

More important than a doctrine of scripture, however, is the

31

need to listen to it, so that it may become part of ourselves and of the way we construe our lives – a purpose a little similar to what Harold Bloom calls for in *How to Read and Why*. According to 1 Peter 1.25, it is the good news, the gospel as it is proclaimed, which is the word of God. An important element of the question, therefore, is the relation which the scriptures bear to the gospel as it is presented to people, and as they hear it. The Jesus of the road to Emmaus was able to point the travellers to the scriptures for them to find meaning to their predicament only on the basis that they were themselves already steeped in them, and had allowed them to become part of their own identity.

The final part is listening to *ourselves*. We all have thoughts, dreams, wants and experiences. We also have accumulated knowledge, and we are aware of fears and of feelings of anger. Sometimes it can be difficult to know who we are, especially in the light of all we carry – and maybe more so as we grow older. Time spent listening to ourselves is well spent, asking ourselves how we are; Hilaire Belloc's 'The false heart' is probably like many another:

> I said to heart, 'How goes it?' Heart replied:
> 'Right as a Ribstone Pippin.' But it lied.

Many people find it helpful to explore aids to self-awareness such as the Myers-Briggs Type Indicator, which is based on the work of the psychologist C. G. Jung; others are devotees of the 'enneagram'; still others adopt schemes to be unearthed in the analysis of management styles. There is much to be said for all of these, to the extent that they assist the process of self-knowledge and do not become ends in themselves. Similarly, the use of a 'soul friend' or spiritual director can also be helpful – provided we realize, and the 'director' realizes, that their role is not to give or provide direction, but rather to assist us in discovering it for ourselves.

And in it all we listen to *God*. We are told that a high proportion of the British people believe in God; what the surveys do not convey is the nature of the God who attracts such a high following. The God whom Christian people believe in and worship is the God who is embodied in Jesus. This Jesus is no longer embodied, for he has ascended to the Father, but we may read him in the scriptures, recognize him in the breaking of the bread, meet him in our neighbour, serve him in the stranger and grow to imitate him as we act in such a way as will make real the kingdom of God in the life of our culture. Listening is one of the means we have of doing all of that; to fail to listen is to risk the state of affairs pictured in the poem of Stevie Smith, 'Not waving but drowning', in which nobody hears the dead man, who (paradoxically) still lies moaning, telling the bystanders that he was *much further out* than they thought, 'And not waving but drowning'. They sympathize and assume that he must have become so cold that his heart gave way. He responds with sad resignation:

> Oh, no no no, it was too cold always
> (Still the dead one lay moaning)
> I was much too far out all my life
> And not waving but drowning.

————•◆•————

Questions

- When have you been listened to?
- What training have you received in listening?
- What aspects of our culture do you find agreeable with the good news of Jesus Christ?
- What aspects of our culture do you find in contradiction to the good news of Jesus Christ?
- Do you like people?

- What power do you have – at work, at home, in church affairs? Are you accountable?
- How much time do you spend reading the Bible?
- Has God ever spoken to you?

4

Serving

Reading
John 13.1–15

Now before the festival of the Passover, Jesus knew that his hour had come to depart from this world and go to the Father. Having loved his own who were in the world, he loved them to the end. The devil had already put it into the heart of Judas son of Simon Iscariot to betray him. And during supper Jesus, knowing that the Father had given all things into his hands, and that he had come from God and was going to God, got up from the table, took off his outer robe, and tied a towel around himself. Then he poured water into a basin and began to wash the disciples' feet and to wipe them with the towel that was tied around him. He came to Simon Peter, who said to him, 'Lord, are you going to wash my feet?' Jesus answered, 'You do not know now what I am doing, but later you will understand.' Peter said to him, 'You will never wash my feet.' Jesus answered, 'Unless I wash you, you have no share with me.' Simon Peter said to him, 'Lord, not my feet only but also my hands and my head!' Jesus said to him, 'One who has bathed does not need to wash, except for the feet, but is entirely clean. And you are clean, though not all of you.' For he knew who was to betray him; for this reason he said, 'Not all of you are clean.'

After he had washed their feet, had put on his robe, and had returned to the table, he said to them, 'Do you know what I have done to you? You call me Teacher and Lord – and you are right, for that is what I am. So if I, your Lord and Teacher, have washed your feet, you also ought to wash one another's feet. For I have set you an example, that you also should do as I have done to you.'

Text
Luke 22.27

'I am among you as one who serves.'

———•◆•———

As we saw, the first two talents we discussed, looking and listening, are by no means passive forms of behaviour. The subject of this chapter, *serving*, is perhaps more obviously not. At the root of this word in Greek is the sense of *dust*: a servant is one who works 'through dust, or ashes'. In this chapter we look at two Gospel passages; they seem to be telling the same story, but their focuses are different. It is possible that St Luke's Gospel influences St John's in some way; it is certainly curious how they both handle the subject of 'service' at the Last Supper.

We look first at Luke. I have always been amused by the story at the start of Acts 6 about the decision of the apostles to appoint 'seven men of good standing', to 'serve tables' (or, perhaps, to 'add up the figures, do the bookkeeping'). The very thing which the apostles felt to be beneath their dignity in Acts, Jesus implies in Luke is his characteristic way of being: 'I am among you as one who serves'.

The whole panorama of the Lucan story has developed to this point, and we are about to enter upon the last earthly days of Jesus. The structure of Luke 22 involves a piling up of episodes in the interaction between Jesus and the disciples; the style is as jittery as the disciples, and one can sense the general nervousness. They come to eat the Passover, and this leads not to a sense of unity, as Christian people might hope, but to what appears at first sight to be a struggle for power; after this episode, Jesus tells Peter that Satan is to lead him astray and cause him to deny that he knows him; he tells the disciples to ensure that they have with them purse, bag, sandals and sword; and then they go off to face the uncertain future.

Perhaps we can excuse the apostles in Acts 6 if we note the context in Luke 22, for that is one of suffering, and the disciples are afraid. The question posed by James and John immediately after the words over the bread and the cup and the unspecific prophecy of his denial might appear to be motivated by the desire for power; but perhaps it is panic. Will everything be all right? Will the kingdom come (just as the disciples ask Jesus in Acts 1.6, 'Lord, is this the time when you will restore the kingdom to Israel?')? Will *we* be all right? Has this been a sensible way to spend this past period of our lives? It is interesting to note that the passage in 1 Peter 5.6–7, which exhorts its readers to humility, 'humble yourselves therefore under the mighty hand of God', proceeds to deal with their anxiety: 'cast all your anxiety on him, because he cares for you'. Maybe there is connection between anxiety and the desire to be honoured. Jesus points out that the disciples have remained with him in his trials, and he promises that they will be rewarded. His trials have been theirs, and theirs are his, and the same will be true of the glory that is to follow. What they are seeking is reassurance, and maybe James and John speak for the rest of the disciples.

Luke takes the story from Mark 10 in which the disciples James and John are elbowing for position in the coming kingdom – where Jesus is assumed to have some standing. It is interesting to note that they have clearly managed to pick up that much of what he has told them! They are Christ-centred in their assumptions, but not in their behaviour. It is worth recalling that convictions about Jesus have to be internalized and acted out, not just recited, parrot-fashion. What is striking about Luke's positioning of the story, as distinct from Mark's, is that the conversation takes place in the context of the eating of the Passover and immediately after the institution of the Lord's Supper, whereas for Mark it was in the context of what Jesus says about discipleship after being asked by a rich young man what he should do to inherit eternal life. Following Jesus, he is told, is costly. The disciples point out that they have left everything in order to follow Jesus, and he says they will be rewarded in the kingdom of God. He emphasizes that they will share his sufferings, and James and John make their request immediately after this saying. This snippet of conversation sits a little awkwardly there, and maybe Luke is attempting to provide a more fitting context for it.

In response to the disciples' anxiety, Jesus points out that the only proper approach to people is service; he makes a commonplace observation about being a servant – 'for who is greater, the one who is at the table or the one who serves? Is it not the one at the table?' – and states his own model: 'But I am among you as one who serves.' Then he reassures them of their place in the coming kingdom, telling them that they will have authority to judge the 12 tribes of Israel. Such an idea is prevalent in contemporary apocalyptic literature; it either means that they will exercise the final judgement on behalf of God over the nation of Israel, or that they will rule over the nation, as did those whose stories are told in the Book of Judges in the Old Testament. Whatever the correct interpretation may be, we can say that Jesus assures them that this pain will be redeemed.

It is difficult to grasp this, but the point is that we are called to serve, even though we ourselves are in pain. Do you remember Ally McBeal, that crazy, loveable, infuriating – and almost pathologically anxious – lawyer in the television series? In particular, do you recall the conversation she has with the ghost of Billy Thomas? 'Have you seen God yet?' Humour surfaces in Billy's cautious response, 'There are certain conditions about confidentiality.' Ally continues, 'When you see him, will you tell him how much I hate him?'

Billy's death had to happen (and we fanatics who had visited the website before the broadcast knew that it was going to). Yes, the relationship had been as cookie as the characters. Ally and Billy had been childhood sweethearts; they had gone on to Law School at Harvard together; and they graduated. But then Billy decided to leave Ally and move away in order to further his career. They met again when Ally went to work for a new law firm, where Billy was now a partner – but he was now also the married partner of Georgia.

This happened; that happened; Billy and Georgia split up; Billy started having hallucinations; then, one day, after collapsing in the courthouse and publicly swearing to Ally, 'love, all love, for ever, stronger than death', he announced that he was tired, sat down on the floor and died of a brain haemorrhage. His ghost later visits Ally in her office, and they speak about heaven: 'Have you seen God yet? . . . When you see him, will you tell him how much I hate him?'

Ally's pain means that she has a valid case against God. And so do the parents of children killed in war. Along with the relatives of the victims of terrorist atrocities. And those involved in natural disasters and train crashes. And the innumerable fathers and mothers, daughters and sons, sisters and brothers, friends and lovers of those suddenly killed in violent acts or in accidents, or unexpectedly taken ill and rushed off for surgery. 'Have you seen God yet? When you see him, will you tell him how much I hate him?' Hating God is one possible response to our pain.

However, there is another possibility. In *The London Review of Books* a couple of years ago, Ian Hacking recalled an incident on the London Underground:

In 1972, I was on the London Underground when a man failed to mind the gap. Not only did he put his foot between the train and the platform, but he did so as the train was starting; he was dragged a short distance before the train was halted, and his leg was pulled downwards. He was in agony, his leg torn and he could not extricate it from the gap. Someone, a station guard or a commuter, took charge. 'Lean against the carriage and lift it!' he shouted. We did. 'One, two, three – heave.' We heaved and held. It is quite surprising how high you can lift an Underground carriage if the lot of you give it body and soul for a short time. The man was helped out, the emergency services arrived, and we all went our different ways.

We are not told how Ian Hacking was feeling that morning, nor whether any of those commuters on the platform had shouted at their partners over breakfast, failed to say their prayers, or were thinking lustful thoughts about their office colleagues. Nor do we know how many of them were in mourning, how many had only recently been told they had but a few weeks to live, how many were themselves suffering pain. But we are told a parable of the kingdom of God. And it is just possible that the victim of the accident might have decided, in spite of his pain – and in a curious way, as a result of it – that he loved the human race that morning, because, as Christians would put it, he had seen the God and Father of Jesus Christ incarnate in the behaviour of his neighbours.

If we note, not so much the childishness of James and John, but their fear and anxiety, and the maturity and wisdom of Jesus, we might learn that the fear of the absence of status, or of the loss of it, is nothing when set against the possibility of getting a life. And that will be achieved only by taking on the fears that come our way, the aches, 'the thousand natural shocks that flesh is heir to', and not passing the buck of our pain further down the line to our families, our colleagues and our neighbours.

The passage in John 13 seems to be a development of what happens in Luke 22; maybe it is this hint in Luke of 'being among [them] as one who serves' which evokes John's story of Jesus washing the feet of the disciples in the upper room. Luke does not tell us what the serving is of which Jesus speaks, and so leaves us to figure out that his service might have to do with his sacrifice. The truly startling thing is that, while in Luke 22 we have focused on the disciples' anxiety and pain, the one who is really to suffer is Jesus himself. That is why John says, 'Jesus, knowing that the Father had given all things into his hands, and that he had come from God and was going to God, got up from the table, took off his outer robe, and tied a towel around himself. Then he poured water into a basin and began to wash the disciples' feet and to wipe them with the towel that was tied around him.'

The action of Jesus in this act of service is made in full consciousness of what is about to happen to him, and is something truly mundane and necessary to their comfort. He washes the dust from their feet. In *The Secret Life of Dust* (John Wiley & Sons, NY, 2001), Hannah Holmes tells the story of dust, this 'sparkly fuzzy stuff', as she calls it:

> Too small to distinguish are the individual fragments of a disintegrating world: the skin flakes, rock flecks, tree bark, bicycle paint, lampshade fibers, ant legs, sweater wool, brick shards, tire rubber, hamburger soot, and bacteria . . . The world is in a constant state of disintegration.

Holmes goes on to tell us that dust is measured in microns – and a micron is one twenty-five-thousandth of an inch. The width of the average human hair is 100 microns, and a piece of hair 100 microns long is too large to be regarded as dust; it is sand. Fungal spores measure between one and five microns; pollen between ten and 100, and stardust one tenth.

It is in dust that the universe has its origin. As particles of dust melted and coalesced, so worlds were formed in the spiralling heat of creative energy. We are constituted out of the basic elements that came into being in that heat, and we grow as we take these in from the natural world we inhabit.

It is dust that keeps the universe in balance. Water vapour collects around particles of dust; fungi, blown all over the planet, break down both solid rock and the dead flesh of animals; pollens catch the wind to continue the cycle of reproduction in greenery and plants.

And dust will feature in the process in which the universe will disintegrate. Dinosaurs have already disappeared, thanks to dust, and before the final conflagration dust will blow again across the hot earth, adding to the destruction of whatever life there might be at that time.

The servant, the one who helps, is the 'by dust' person, and in the middle of all of it. The task of the servant is all to do with clearing out the fireplace and sweeping the house; so the image is of Cinderella. Buttons in the pantomime is talking to you and me when he says, 'Hello, Cinders!'

The role of the servant is basic to the functioning of the Church. Servants are mentioned in Philippians 1.1, in 1 Timothy 3 and in Ignatius of Antioch; and the seven men chosen in Acts 7 to do the work which the apostles thought beneath their dignity have come to be called 'deacons' because they 'served tables': either as waiters or as accountants. Max Thurian, in *Priesthood and Ministry: Ecumenical Research* (Mowbray, London, 1983), talks about apostles, bishops, presbyters and then deacons, top down, but Christian faith is bottom up: 'I am among you as one who serves.'

Washing feet is a slave's job. What is significant here is that it is the host, the Master, who performs this dirty and demeaning task. And he does it for a purpose: '. . . if I, your Lord and [Master], have washed your feet, you also ought to wash one another's feet'. He subverts the roles of 'lord' and 'master', behaving like a slave to his disciples, in order to leave them an example, that they should follow in his steps.

Slaves retain their position as slaves, he says, and the statement, 'Slaves are not greater than their master, nor are messengers greater than the one who sent them', parallels the saying in Luke 22, 'For who is greater, the one who is at the table or the one who serves? Is it not the one at the table?' Here the disciples have a model of how to behave towards each other: '. . . if I, your Lord and [Master], have washed your feet, you also ought to wash one another's feet'. For St John, Jesus is the Logos of God who has become flesh, and now walks the earth; that is to say, he is the rational and creative principle at the heart of all things, and the mind of all people, and the sense of order and beauty and creativity. There is therefore no human development to be seen in Jesus in John's Gospel as there is in the Synoptic Gospels; Jesus knows that the Father has given all things into his hands, and that he has come from God and is going to God. He knows of the treachery of Judas. He knows all about the pain which the coming days will bring. He takes hold of all that bloody future – 'knowing all things' – and gets up from the table, takes off his outer robe, ties a towel around himself, pours water into a basin and begins to wash the disciples' feet and to wipe them with the towel.

Service, or helping, is the start, the foundation of any Christian ministry – indeed the words mean the same! This is the case, first, because there is little we have to offer by way of 'ministry' to people if we do not love people and want to help them; it is also true, second, because service contains within it the seeds of the gospel, for this act of servanthood also has something to say about sacrifice.

Serving has something to do with sacrifice because sacrifice has to do with the act of sanctifying, of making holy – that is the meaning of the word – of what we have at our disposal. This is a most important lesson, for here lies the possibility of forgiveness, and therefore of understanding, and therefore of living. The whole point of sacrifice is making holy; it is not, primarily, giving up; it is sanctifying. No doubt we are aware that the more we devote ourselves to God, the more precious to us will be the offerings which we make in sacrifice to him.

The curious thing is that Jesus here has nothing to offer; he is about to go to his death. What are we to make of that? Could it be that he makes an offering of that very fact – that he is about to go to his death? Maybe he makes an offering of his pain. This calls for some reflection. It couldn't be, could it, that we cherish our pain as one of our most precious possessions? Is it that our pain is the last thing we are able to let go? Do we – even against our own will and judgement, sometimes – hold to *this* at all costs? And if it is so, could it be because we expect other people to minister to *us* in our suffering? Do we, somehow, treasure *this* among the most prized of our possessions? One of the pleasures of holding on to our pain is that of doling it out to other people as we will.

I suspect that, at some time or another, many of us have not only wallowed in misery but also enjoyed the fantasies to which our disappointments and our anger give rise. We have hoped for revenge, indulged in nostalgia, wallowed in regret and enjoyed a perverted sense of 'not being happy unless we are miserable' (a condition which we usually ascribe to other people).

In getting up from table to serve, to help, simply to wash his disciples' feet, Jesus begins the sacrifice of what is to happen to him. He makes of it an offering, he makes it holy; and here begins the unfolding of the plan of the world's forgiveness.

And there is something else, a further thing, for he also shows us here something about our identity. There echoes constantly in the stories of Jesus throughout all the Gospels the question, 'Who is he?' This question is not absent here. The narratives of his birth, found in Matthew and Luke, which include the angels, the shepherds and the wise men from the East, do not explain who he is; they are a way of asserting his significance in the plans of God for the world. The stories of Mary and Joseph, of

Herod and the flight to Egypt, of Simeon and Anna, and of the incident in the Temple, all express the early Christian community's conviction that he is more than merely human; there is an added dimension to his being which has us humans groping for metaphors and verbal images in order to put into words our inability to describe him.

This is because it is impossible to speak about him except in terms which also require that we speak about ourselves. Closely bound up with the story of Jesus is always the question of the ways in which his disciples related to him. So here he tells Peter that he can have no part in him unless he wash him; he speaks of the necessity of following his example; and he spells out that the only valid evidence of the disciples' relationship with him will be their love. So the relationship between him and them suggests that it is also appropriate to ask, 'Who are *they*?' And then, because of the kind of answers that are on offer, and because the whole story is written for our learning: because, in other words, the question of discipleship takes in the reader, we present-day readers find the question developing into, 'Who am I?'

It is tempting to say that the role of the disciples here focuses on following him, on imitation. Such a view would not be wholly wrong; but the matter goes deeper than that, for it is in our discipleship and our following that we become who we are. Our identity depends upon our meeting and identification with Jesus.

The reason for this is that the washing which Jesus offers in this story – and in the Church's sacrament of baptism – is not primarily about being clean; it is about being included. That explains Peter's problem. His refusal to have his feet washed can easily be explained, either as excessive humility: 'I cannot have *you* washing *me*, Lord!'; or as a kind of religiosity that is almost nauseating: 'O well, Lord, if you must wash me, then I need to be washed all over, for I feel so filthy!'

Cleanness is a metaphor for inclusion. And this is a genuine inclusion; we really do all belong, and we belong together, for he washes us all. There is no room for any exclusivism around this table; we are one human race, and all of us belong to Christ. All are welcome, because he is the one, inclusive Son of man, Son of God, human being. Being included *by* him, being identified *with* him, being incorporated *in* him – is our destiny, our identity.

'Do you understand what I have done for you?', he asks. I suspect that we both understand and fail to. On the one hand there is a sense in which we can say, 'Yes, we see what you mean; you walked the way of service and of sacrifice and so became who you are, the Son of God, by obedience in the things that you suffered; and we can see that the invitation is to walk the same way, of service and of identification with your suffering, so that we too become who we are and discover our identity in identifying ourselves with you.' But on the other hand we shrink from the demands that such an understanding entails. The pain we have we would rather keep, so that we can dish it out again in turn to those who afflict us; and as for our identity, we would rather remain hidden within the subterfuges of our *personae*, our masks, in the counterfeit existences provided by the defences we put up; we do not want other people to see our true, vulnerable selves.

So our learning continues; but this story in John 13 of his serving the disciples reminds us that the sacrifice of Jesus, made in full awareness of his own identity, makes both for our forgiveness and therefore also for our discovery of who we are. The good news of Jesus Christ is an invitation, a hint, a proposal, to accompany this man on his walk through the holy lands of our lives, and to explore with him, not, primarily, where we might *find* comfort and help – though, God knows, we need them – but where we might *offer* them, so that the bitterness of life might not become cancerous to our souls.

And the point of all this is not that we should spend our time pretending that we are special and congratulating ourselves because we have been redeemed, forgiven and saved; but that we should get on with the business of living redeemed, forgiven and salvific lives; that is, lives which are concerned with providing ways by which our neighbours may come to health and wholeness. That means helping them through their pain.

One implication of that is that we are not there to pass judgement. We are often guilty of collusion with a 'culture of complaint' (to use Robert Hughes' phrase): people don't go to church; people don't think; people don't join things; children play with computers rather than train sets, as God intended; people watch too much television; people listen to personal stereos, which shows how society has become privatized . . . And so on.

It could be that we need to get off their backs, because they are in pain.

The parable of that possibility is acted out on the Christian altar. Here we bring together and offer what we are given and what we make of it – 'which earth has given and human hands have made': bread and fruit; labour and skill – along with joy and pain; and it is all made holy by God's blessing of it, and then returned to us entirely gracious, life-giving and redemptive.

'Have you seen God yet? . . . When you see him, will you tell him how much I hate him?'

God responds to that hate by washing our feet, demonstrating a love that transcends our hatred and our pain, and transfiguring them into a capacity to love our neighbour and to build a new world, and so exemplifying the principle that we are invited to be among people in the world as those who serve.

———•◆•———

Questions

- Whom do you hate?
- Who loves you?
- What acts of service have you performed today?
- What experience have you had in the past week of being served?

5

Growing Up

Reading
Genesis 3.1–19

Now the serpent was more crafty than any other wild animal that the LORD God had made. He said to the woman, 'Did God say, "You shall not eat from any tree in the garden"?' The woman said to the serpent, 'We may eat of the fruit of the trees in the garden; but God said, "You shall not eat of the fruit of the tree that is in the middle of the garden, nor shall you touch it, or you shall die."' But the serpent said to the woman, 'You will not die; for God knows that when you eat of it your eyes will be opened, and you will be like God, knowing good and evil.' So when the woman saw that the tree was good for food, and that it was a delight to the eyes, and that the tree was to be desired to make one wise, she took of its fruit and ate; and she also gave some to her husband, who was with her, and he ate. Then the eyes of both were opened, and they knew that they were naked; and they sewed fig leaves together and made loincloths for themselves.

They heard the sound of the LORD God walking in the garden at the time of the evening breeze, and the man and his wife hid themselves from the presence of the LORD God among the trees of the garden. But the LORD God called to the man, and said to him, 'Where are you?' He said, 'I heard the sound of you in the garden, and I was afraid, because I was naked; and I hid myself.' He said, 'Who told you that you were naked? Have you eaten from the tree of which I commanded you not to eat?' The man said, 'The woman whom you gave to be with me, she gave me fruit from the tree, and I ate.' Then the LORD God said to the woman, 'What is this that you have done?' The woman said, 'The serpent tricked me, and I ate.' The LORD God said to the serpent,

'Because you have done this, cursed are you among all animals and among all wild creatures; upon your belly you shall go, and dust you shall eat all the days of your life. I will put enmity between you and the woman, and between your offspring and hers; he will strike your head, and you will strike his heel.'

To the woman he said,

'I will greatly increase your pangs in childbearing; in pain you shall bring forth children, yet your desire shall be for your husband, and he shall rule over you.'

And to the man he said,

'Because you have listened to the voice of your wife, and have eaten of the tree about which I commanded you, "You shall not eat of it," cursed is the ground because of you; in toil you shall eat of it all the days of your life; thorns and thistles it shall bring forth for you; and you shall eat the plants of the field. By the sweat of your face you shall eat bread until you return to the ground, for out of it you were taken; you are dust, and to dust you shall return.'

Text

John 8.11

'Neither do I condemn you. Go your way, and from now on do not sin again.'

———•◆•———

A recent, monumental and brilliant study by Terry Eagleton of the idea of the tragic, *Sweet Violence*, suggests that tragedy is not simply a literary category to be regarded as no longer possible because life has become so monochrome, nor to be rejected as undesirable because it is antiquated and élitist; rather it is a category of *life*, closely related to a Christian (and for Eagleton, also a Marxist) identification with the ordinary, the mundane, the everyday. Both Marxism and Christianity seek to redeem tragedy, he says, and they do so 'only by installing themselves at the heart of it' (p. 40). He continues: 'resurrection for Christianity involves a crucifixion and descent into hell. Otherwise what is reclaimed in both cases would not be *this* condition, in all its deadlock and despair'.

Why begin a chapter on 'Growing Up' with a reference to tragedy? First, because tragedy demands a mature response on the part of human beings; and second, because it may provide a means – and this has to be stated very tentatively and very carefully: it may provide a means by which we can allow ourselves to grow. Tragedy demands a mature response, because the alternative is a constant, childish cycle of recrimination and blame, which can end in destruction; and it provides a means of growth insofar as we are able to transcend what happens to us by forgiving ourselves, our neighbour, the world and God. These things cannot be said lightly, because tragedy is real, and pain is never to be welcomed, and it can be severe. However, the Christian gospel points to a possibility of the transformation of our experience, and this is always worth exploring.

On the face of it, the reading from Genesis 3 is an aetiological legend which explains why serpents crawl on their bellies – their tongues flicking in and out, appearing to eat the dust – and why humans tend not to like them; why women find labour painful and must expect to be subordinate to men; and why men have to work hard to produce food while also finding work with the soil disagreeable – unless they enjoy gardening.

But read in the light of what we now know about dust (see the previous chapter), the saying is no curse but a simple statement of fact. We, the world and the universe began in dust, continue in dust and shall perish in dust, to be recycled in new formulations of dust as our bodies enter what will simply be another part of the whole process of living and dying.

We also know now that the story in Genesis 3 is not history, but myth, so one way of making sense of it is to ask the obvious literary question about Eve: did she fall or was she pushed? Eve had come from the side of Adam, who is *adamah*, dust. She had refused the easy life of obedience and deference, preferring to take responsibility for her life; and that one action, although it had been forbidden, had been the making of her. In performing it she had become the mother of all daring, of all curiosity. The point at which she 'fell' was not so much the eating of the forbidden fruit as the failure to take responsibility for having done so. Just as feeble Adam blamed her, so she blamed the serpent and turned her back on the possibility of an adult relationship with her God.

We are told in Genesis 1 that the 'LORD God made to grow every tree that is pleasant to the sight and good for food', along with 'the tree of life . . . and the tree of the knowledge of good and evil'. So if God put them there, why did he issue the prohibition against eating from them? Was this some kind of test? Was it for Eve and Adam's good that the command was given? Doesn't God stand in danger of setting up the very state of affairs he wishes to avoid? After all, the knowledge of good and evil is no bad thing, and it is important for human beings to become aware of everything along the whole span of conjecture and experience.

And wasn't the serpent part of the very creation that God had given for Adam to master and cultivate? How come that the creation itself raises questions about the moral framework by which human beings are to live in the world? When he tempts her, Eve explains to the serpent why they are not to eat of it – God has told them that they will die. But why does she add the prohibition against even touching the tree? Does she sense a level of pettiness in the deity, concerning which even the narrator is reticent? (But how can a character in a story know more of what is going on than the narrator?)

Is this a growing child, a person who is becoming aware of conflicting authorities: God's and the serpent's? And interpreting them? By answering the serpent's questions she lays herself open to the discovery that life consists of more than simply doing what she is told. She is learning that she has decisions to take for herself! So the naked, innocent, dependent child is about to clothe herself in responsibility!

So Eve and Adam become human, which is to say, complex and growing up! They learn to question the rule book, and so start on the journey of discovering the world. God, we learn, is concerned about our growth as human beings. And perhaps, after all, he is not asking for blind obedience, but rather ensuring that we grow into mature, discerning adults. The story is all about choices.

But knowledge is not without responsibility. In the Bible, facts entail value, with all the contradictions and complications that reality entails. When God comes looking for him that evening, Adam has the chance to own up to what he has done, and re-establish the relationship. But he misses it, and simply starts the cycle of blame. As happens so very often, events turn out differently from what was expected, and relationships suffer. Knowledge of good and evil – knowledge, *per se* – is necessary and wonderful, but it has consequences which are very mixed.

There is a strand in Christian tradition, going back at least as far as St Augustine, that talks of a 'happy crime, that called for such and so great a redeemer'. It surfaces in that lovely Christmas carol, 'Adam lay ybounden', with the words, 'Ne had the apple taken been, / ne had ever our Lady abeen heavene queen', and in a hymn by Isaac Watts, 'In him [that is, in Christ], the tribes of Adam boast / more blessings than their father lost'.

And of course it is painful, for the knowledge not only is tinged with regret, but it also embraces evil; and of course it is glorious, for the sorrow is not only edged in gold, but cuts to the marrow of human experience.

Did she fall or was she pushed? In one sense she fell, for she and Adam have to live with the responsibility for and the consequences of their actions. However, in another sense she was pushed: pushed to make a choice, pushed to grow up, pushed to recognize that life is messy and chaotic. But it is out of chaos and mess that worlds are created.

Into this world in the process of creation, this very human mix of good confused with evil, comes God in Jesus Christ. He is already there, of course, because God is Spirit and nowhere absent – he is the reflection, the consciousness, the question and the meaning of things. But he comes into it as one of us, as we come into it; to be baffled, amazed, shocked and killed by it. And through all those he comes in order to be raised to life again within it, *that the world might be saved through him.*

The text from St John's Gospel has as its context the free-floating story of 'the woman taken in adultery'. It is found in many manuscripts in John, and in others in Luke, and is clearly an intrusion into the text wherever it is found. Jesus is in the Temple teaching, when he is interrupted by the scribes and Pharisees who say that the woman they set before him has been caught 'in the very act' of committing adultery. How come, 'in the very act'? We might wonder whether these scribes and Pharisees play the same part as the elders in the story of Susanna, in the Apocrypha, that their voyeurism was so rewarded. In that story two elders spy on Susanna and try to seduce her; failing to do so because she was a virtuous woman, they accuse her publicly of adultery. She is condemned to death, but a man called Daniel – presumably the prophet, the man to whom the Book of Daniel is ascribed – draws the attention of the crowd to the fact that there is no evidence of the woman's adultery other than the witness of the two elders. He asks them separately under which tree they saw her embracing her young lover, and they give different answers. So the two elders are condemned to death, and Susanna and her family rejoice in the justice of God.

Clearly the Pharisees in this story knew where to find the woman; but isn't it strange that there is no mention of the man who, presumably, was also caught with her? Perhaps he ran away; or perhaps he didn't exist. It is even tempting to wonder whether, like the lover in the story of Susanna, he was a figment of the fertile imaginations of the Pharisees – *plus ça change!* – except that the narrative demands the woman's guilt.

The scribes and Pharisees quote the Law at Jesus and invite him to comment. Why does he write on the ground? Is this embarrassment? Is it him not knowing what to do or how to answer? Is this an ironic mimicry of God's finger having written the Law on the tables of stone that were entrusted to Moses? Is this him giving a new law?

Whatever! It is interesting to note the scribes' and Pharisees' persistence: 'When they kept on questioning him, he straightened up and said . . .' His straightening up is not about enforcing the rule-book; it is about the implacability of the evidence of their own memories: his implicit suggestion – that guilt cannot be restricted to the one individual who has the misfortune to get caught – leaves them with nothing further to do but quietly to withdraw, like her lover. So Jesus is left alone with the woman to utter the verdict he has been invited to pronounce. Even though those who asked him for it have gone away, he still makes his pronouncement; and that pronouncement is of an unconditional forgiveness, coupled with a word that liberates the woman from the necessity of both living with guilt and continuing such a life.

Who is she, alone in the guilt of what can only ever be a shared crime? Another Eve, perhaps, who remains nameless until after the story of her disobedience? This woman is never named at all. Another difference would be that Eve was 'proactive', as we would say, while this woman, at least when we meet her, has lost any initiative she may have taken earlier. Here she is done to rather than doing.

Might we set the stones of the Temple in which the story is set, over against the stones which the self-righteous want to cast at the offender? And when it says that Jesus wrote 'on the ground', 'on the earth', are we justified in seeing the dust there? In that environment, of course, much of the dust would be from those very stones. This woman has been disobedient, like Eve. But unlike Eve she casts no blame, neither on a serpent nor on an absent lover.

And Jesus rewrites the rules. No vengeful, protective gardener he, nor one for throwing tablets of stone about; so in the dust of the ground the finger of the Son of God writes down the new law of the woman's forgiveness and freedom. 'Neither do I condemn you. Go your way, and sin no more.' In other words, though you are dust, and though you came from dust, and though you will return to dust, will you allow yourself to realize the image of God that you bear – and, indeed, will you be deified by the divine goodness? Will you dare to be dust that aspires to be diamond, graced by God to grow up and share in the creation of new worlds of beauty and of love? If so, the way towards that is for you to admit to whatever responsibility is yours for what happens: in the gardens and in the bedrooms – your own or anybody else's – and even in the Temples, in which you try to hide.

To be a Christian individual or community is to mediate the possibility of such a growing up. According to 1 Peter 2.9 the Christian community is a 'royal priesthood'. Some people refer to this idea as the priesthood of all believers, others as the priesthood of the Church. The two terms are not mutually exclusive: they bear witness to an important aspect of the Church's life. The English word 'priest' comes from a Greek word that means 'older person'. So from a linguistic point of view there is an association of priesthood with seniority and maturity; the image could be of an older sister or brother sorting out the squabbles of younger siblings and smoothing things over with the parents. Older people, with their maturity, are expected to be grown up enough to know that only by forgiveness can the world function. The priesthood of the individual in the Christian community derives from the priesthood of the whole people of God; we take on an intercessory role on behalf of humanity; and, most particularly, with the insight provided us in the gospel, we focus on the possibility of change, of transformation, of forgiveness, of restoration.

A maturity about this will remind us of a point that Harry Williams makes (in *The True Wilderness*, Constable & Company, London, 1965), to the effect that, when everything is taken into consideration, when we look over all that we know, all that we experience, all that we observe in the lives of those we know, when all is said and done, we are more sinned against than sinning. It will put us in the position to see that this is the way things are. To assert that there is a difference between right and wrong is not the same as saying that they are easy to distinguish in all circumstances; and we often have to live with the accusation that we are, to all intents and purposes, blurring the distinctions.

But the important point is that we are in a position to be gracious, both to ourselves and to neighbours; and we have no alternative but to take responsibility for our behaviour – and that will include forgiveness. We have to forgive because we ourselves are also implicated in wrongdoing; we are not in full possession of the facts nor are we party to the wrongdoer's feelings. Moreover, the consequences of not forgiving may be worse than we thought, the relationship might be more important than the sin, and it is only by forgiveness that people can learn to love more.

Certainly, we cannot allow ourselves 'the luxury of a clear conscience'; but we might seriously cultivate a community of forgiveness.

Is a 'reclamation' possible in this desperate, deadlocked world? Maybe we are inclined to think, 'No; it's over the top; it's too bad; it's gone too far.' I have a friend who left the priesthood for a while because he decided he no longer believed it all; but he came back to it when he realized that there was nowhere else where he could find forgiveness written into the structure of the institution; and a contemporary of mine in ordination training – a food scientist who later became the doyen of ministry in secular employment – used to say after every food scare that came along (salmonella, listeria, whatever) that perfection was impossible, and everybody knew it; what was needed was for the food industry to know about forgiveness.

But perhaps it is precisely our thinking 'No' that provides us with a seed of hope. The last thing that the world needed in the spring of 2003 was a war with Iraq. Early in 2001 the global economy already was beginning to slump; then there was the shock of 11 September 2001; then we heard that the Americans were going to invade Afghanistan – and they did; then, not surprisingly, the economic indicators which were already shaky before that dreadful day continued to produce bad news; then we heard that the Americans were determined to invade Iraq; then we heard that the British Prime Minister was inclined to help him; and now the reasons for doing so appear to be less and less plausible. And so the whole tragedy unfolded before us like a real-time Tom and Jerry – except that people really were getting killed.

Over against the elements of our suffering and our present sense of tragedy, Christian people set the person and character of Jesus Christ. And I say that not to offer a simple, pious, world-denying solution, but to suggest that we explore a profound, worldly and even complex one.

Do we fear terrorism? Do we fear nuclear and chemical weapons, especially if they are in the hands of those who might want to attack us? Or do we fear that the war will escalate beyond what the coalition is able to control?

Are we afraid of the prospect of tyranny and the end of our civilization? Or is it the prospect of an American-led tyranny, if not of oppression and injustice, then of a mind-numbing Bush-style Americanization and – given all the moral ambiguities of US foreign policy in recent decades – the exercise of unaccountable economic power and manipulation?

Do we regret the casualties that war inevitably brings? Do we lament the death of truth, the first casualty of war?

Do we feel a sense of shame that there is not greater support for the war on the part of those who benefit from freedoms which the Iraqi people cannot enjoy? Or do we have a sense of shame, that we have been brought to this pass, attacking a Muslim state precisely when we need to listen to and learn from the aspirations of Muslims and, indeed, all those other people whose cultures differ from our own?

True, we have not yet resisted to the point of shedding our blood; but we fear we might yet have to. But fear, death, loss of truth, shame: all of these are found in the story of Jesus. They are found and addressed and redeemed; because Jesus is at the heart of it all. The Christian redemption of tragedy, to paraphrase Eagleton, is brought about 'by installing Christ at the heart of it'.

It is, of course, God who instals himself as Christ at the heart of it. So it is there, when the impossibility of the situation is owned and faced, that the possibility lies of transformation and forgiveness. And that comes with an openness to all that God may allow for us, however grim. This is not a challenge to an impossible task. If the tragedy is 'one thing on top of another', like successive waves of B52 bombers, so is the grace of God. To grow up is to recognize the complexity of things. It is not to have all the answers, but to live with the reality that the answers are not there to be had. To walk 'by faith and not by sight' is to live with all the deadlock and despair of tragedy and to transfigure them by seeing Christ at the heart of it all; that is what it is to be in the process of growing up.

———•◆•———

Questions

- Sharing our private fears and our sense of guilt is something we can only do in the context of close and safe relationships. What networks do you have that enable you to be honest about the things which sadden or haunt you?
- The present Archbishop of Canterbury opened his Enthronement Sermon in February 2003 by telling his hearers that somebody had once said that if someone came up to you in the street and whispered, 'They've found out! Run!', most of us would. Would you?
- What makes you angry?
- Does being older necessarily mean being wiser?

6

Speaking

Reading
Isaiah 61.1–11

The spirit of the Lord GOD is upon me, because the LORD has anointed me; he has sent me to bring good news to the oppressed, to bind up the broken-hearted, to proclaim liberty to the captives, and release to the prisoners; to proclaim the year of the LORD's favour, and the day of vengeance of our God; to comfort all who mourn; to provide for those who mourn in Zion – to give them a garland instead of ashes, the oil of gladness instead of mourning, the mantle of praise instead of a faint spirit. They will be called oaks of righteousness, the planting of the LORD, to display his glory. They shall build up the ancient ruins, they shall raise up the former devastations; they shall repair the ruined cities, the devastations of many generations.

Strangers shall stand and feed your flocks, foreigners shall till your land and dress your vines; but you shall be called priests of the LORD, you shall be named ministers of our God; you shall enjoy the wealth of the nations, and in their riches you shall glory. Because their shame was double, and dishonour was proclaimed as their lot, therefore they shall possess a double portion; everlasting joy shall be theirs.

For I the LORD love justice, I hate robbery and wrongdoing; I will faithfully give them their recompense, and I will make an everlasting covenant with them. Their descendants shall be known among the nations, and their offspring among the peoples; all who see them shall acknowledge that they are a people whom the LORD has blessed. I will greatly rejoice in the LORD, my whole being shall exult in my God; for he has clothed me with the garments of salvation, he has covered me with the robe of righteousness, as a bridegroom decks himself with a garland, and as a bride adorns herself with her jewels.

For as the earth brings forth its shoots, and as a garden causes what is sown in it to spring up, so the Lord GOD will cause righteousness and praise to spring up before all the nations.

Text

Luke 4.21

Then he began to say to them, 'Today this scripture has been fulfilled in your hearing.'

————•◆•————

What might it mean – and what might it be like – to be *breathed on* by God?

Perhaps you think that it would be nice and comfortable. Legend has it that otters used to breathe on St Cuthbert in order to dry him after he had spent the night praying in the sea. If that is the image that comes to your mind in response to the question, then you would be consoled by the warmth.

Or perhaps you think that you wouldn't survive the heat. After all, 'our God is a consuming fire', we are told in Hebrews 12.29; and 2 Thessalonians 2.8 tells of the time when 'the lawless one will be revealed, whom the Lord Jesus will destroy with the breath of his mouth, annihilating him by the manifestation of his coming'. If that is the image, then you would be consumed by the fire!

The word 'spirit' comes from a Latin word meaning 'to breathe'; so the 'Spirit' of God is the *breath* of God; and the prophet speaks of having the Spirit of God upon him as a result of his anointing to bring good news, to preach and to proclaim.

So this breath is associated neither with warmth nor with scorching heat, but with language. That suggestion might remind us of the story of creation in Genesis 1, when the Spirit of God hovers over watery chaos, until God utters the words which bring about the creation, first, of light, to enable him to see what he is doing; then of the heavens and the earth; then of the waters and of the dry land; then of all that lives in them – until finally he creates an image for himself: humankind.

It is language that brings it all about; and right from the start the language is good news. 'God saw everything that he had made, and indeed, it was very good.'

The passage from Isaiah 61 is a prophecy from the third section of the Book of Isaiah about the destiny of Jerusalem after the return of the people from exile in Babylon. And it is fascinating to note the extent of the metaphors which it contains. As we have said, 'Spirit' is breath, and this is God's breath – whatever that might be! The prophet has been anointed – that is, he has had oil poured on him; but this has been done by God – however that might have happened! And the metaphorical oil bears the divine breath, so that the prophet may say what God wants him to say.

What God wants him to say is that in the new Jerusalem which will be established after the people have returned from exile there will be solace for the brokenhearted, there will be liberty for those who formerly were captives in Babylon, and there will be release for prisoners. The future will be one great, continuous Jubilee year, a year of the Lord's favour.

However, the imagery of the year gives way to the imagery of the day, for this will be a day of vengeance to be wreaked by God upon those who made his people suffer – which might be considered curious, since it was God, say the prophets before the exile, including Isaiah of Jerusalem, who sent the people to Babylon as punishment for their disobedience. Nevertheless, the word is of comfort for all in Zion who mourn. They will be given garlands instead of ashes, the oil of gladness instead of mourning, the mantle of praise instead of a faint spirit. Such was the language of the return from exile for inhabitants of Judah who had been led away captive to Babylon in 587 BCE. Their return would be a time of unforgettable and almost unimaginable rejoicing.

The imagery is also of the conquest of other nations. Verse 5, 'Strangers shall stand and feed your flocks, foreigners shall till your land and dress your vines; but you shall be called priests of the LORD, you shall be named ministers of our God; you shall enjoy the wealth of the nations, and in their riches you shall glory.' The 'dirty work' would be left to mere foreigners, while the nation of Israel would swan around like the idle rich, never doing a stroke of work.

If it all sounds a bit unreal, that might have something to do with the fact that it did not, in fact, come about. The resettlement of Judea after the Exile represented far more problems than the imagination of the prophet was capable of expressing – for all that his prophecies were gathered together in a text which combined those of Isaiah of Jerusalem, who predicted the start of the Exile, with those of 'Second Isaiah', who predicted its end.

After their return from Exile, the nation was part of the confusion which was Judea in those centuries prior to the rise of Alexander the Great, the break-up of his empire in the Hellenistic period, and the coming of the Romans in the century before Christ. *The Lord God* did not *cause righteousness and praise to spring up before all the nations*!

The Gospel according to St Luke takes up this sense of unfulfilment and – by the creative power of its language – brings about a new state of affairs. Central to the story is the claim of Jesus, *'Today this scripture has been fulfilled in your hearing'*, even though the point of the story does not end there.

Luke expands the simple statement to be found in Mark, that Jesus went preaching in the synagogues of his home region, and creates a new narrative. Jesus is full of the Spirit, not only because he has been baptized, and because he is the descendant of Adam, the son of God, but also because, with the appropriate use of the scriptures, he has overcome particular temptations. He might have turned stones into bread, so manufacturing artificial manna to feed himself and the people in the wilderness; he might have made himself content to worship that which was other than God, in order to gain the kingdoms of the world on diabolical terms; he might have thrown himself down from the pinnacle of the Temple in Jerusalem in order to demonstrate that God was with him, without the cross, without the shame, without any pain, without any possibility of the transfiguration of the human lot.

However, for Luke's Jesus, to be filled with the *breath* of God means inspiration with a new language of the *kingdom* of God, which is present to those who hear him and which makes claims upon them. The concept of 'fulfilment' is created by the recollection of the sense of 'incompleteness' which it presupposes. This process can be seen with our understanding of Jesus as the Christ. The New Testament scholar Leslie Houlden suggested some time ago that the name, or title, 'Christ' was nowhere near as popular and prevalent in the time of Jesus and the early Church as many Christian exegetes would suggest. Houlden combed the literature and came to the conclusion that the concept arose *at the same time* as the conviction that the Christ was none other than Jesus risen from the dead.

Jesus neither 'filled' a ready-made 'Christ-shaped' slot, nor took on a familiar concept and reinvented it; rather, the early Christians came to view the risen Jesus as God's anointed one, God's Son and chosen king. In naming him 'Christ' they invented a concept and filled it out with allusions to the Jewish scriptures and so gave shape to title, concept and person in one go.

This is what is happening in Luke 4. The Gospels were written after the resurrection, of course, and here the tradition is being told anew, rewritten in the light of the experience of Jesus as alive within the context of his age. For Luke, Jesus *is* good news for the poor; that is, those outside, those who are disregarded, those who are considered beyond the pale. For Luke, Jesus is not so much shaping an old tradition as creating something new and using the tradition to explore what that might mean.

Does Jesus' quotation of the part of Isaiah 61 imply his adoption of the whole? Or is the absence of any talk of 'conquest' the cause of the people's rejection of and rage at what he says? What angers them appears to be his suggestion that they are thinking, 'Doctor, cure yourself', along with his reflection that a prophet is not accepted in his own home territory, but that God is not restricted to working among those who pride themselves on being his people.

Such language causes offence to the folk of his home town. The strange thing is that it is his provocation that causes the offence. The sermon was going down well, until he laid into them and suggested that the issue was precisely of how things are today, and here in Nazareth, where he had been brought up. God's good news was free – arbitrary, almost! – and available to outsiders, like the widow of Zarephath in Sidon (cf. the story of Elijah in 1 Kings 17.9ff.) and Naaman the Syrian (cf. the story of Elisha in 2 Kings 5.1ff.). So the Nazarenes had better look to their laurels – even if those 'laurels' are merely the comforts of being resigned to a lack of fulfilment – that state of mind beyond cynicism, which says that promises are never fulfilled, hopes can never be realized, there is no future.

How dare this Jesus come and disturb our ways! What right has this son of someone we know to imply that our religious traditions mean something different from what we have always thought? We must be rid of such a trouble-maker!

We might think that Jesus' escape from the religious lynch-mob is surprising. After all, he came to die, didn't he?, and he was meek and submissive and went to the cross because that is what God required of him. Why then did he not die at this point? After all, he has said what he wants to say!

Maybe the point is that his death, when it comes, is not at the whim of his opponents, but rather at the culmination of the rest of the story. His death is an accomplishment, an achievement. If it is a sentence, it is one spoken and carried out by God himself, with the co-operation of Jesus himself, because it is part of a wider discourse, spoken by the subject himself, who is the bearer of the Spirit of God.

Speaking the good news of the kingdom of God can be a costly business, and it can involve conflict, as Jesus discovered. However, if we are to follow the Spirit of Christ in bearing witness to the kingdom of God, we cannot avoid asking, 'How are we to use the religious traditions at our disposal?' Does our use of them promote freedom, or do we seek to control the lives of other people? Is our witness liberating or is it oppressive? The Jesus of the Synoptic Gospels – and especially of St Luke – is a man with a passion for so interpreting his tradition that it yields its liberating core, its fundamentally generous and open truth, which lies within the heart of a God of infinite and passionate love for all. After what was said in Chapter 2 about Listening, it might be thought that there is nothing to be said. The story of Jesus in the synagogue at Capernaum provides the background to a response to that suggestion. The point is that proclamation takes the context seriously – that is the point of listening; and it is specifically focused upon the kingdom of God.

There are two words which relate to 'preaching' in the New Testament: the first is 'herald', the one who announces the arrival of the king, or who proclaims the king's wishes; the second is 'to announce good news'.

There is no getting away from the fact that the Jesus presented to us in the Synoptic Gospels is a man who has a passion for the reign of God. This was no other-worldly hope, but an insistence that God's rule over the things of earth was to be made real immediately, imminently and here. Its radical demands called into question the reign or rule of any power other than God, and it would issue in an absolute justice, with what has been called a 'bias to the poor'; so it is certainly a justice of politics first of all, and then a justice of the law courts, but ultimately a justice to do with how all people, nations and communities stand before God.

For Luke, Jesus summed up the promises to Israel in a way that read them as intended for the wide world and for the whole of human history. In the end, as we read, Jesus so incenses his hearers that they end up wanting to stone him, but he manages to escape from them.

The task of proclaiming the kingdom of God is to present our hearers with an image of that kingdom which is good news, and which people are entitled to hear as good news. The biblical tradition itself calls us to use the tradition in such a way that we do not simply repeat it, or carry on saying things that we have always said, in the same ways in which we have always said them; rather, that we allow the tradition to inform an insistence that we and our neighbours should hear 'good news' when we speak of Jesus and the kingdom of God – and experience it as such.

This implies that we take some thought about what we say and note the importance of making connections between the results of our looking and listening and the central scriptures of our faith. Our witness to the gospel has to be presented in accessible forms; it requires sensitivity to our hearers. There is also much to be said for taking seriously another point which Harry Williams makes in *The True Wilderness*, when he tells of the decision he made with regard to his preaching, that he would not teach anything that had not become part of his own life and experience. (I once suggested this to a discussion group, and was told that such an approach would not do, because then we would never say anything . . . !) Most important of all, we need to use our imagination creatively in order to present to people a Jesus who is credible and whose presence is good news.

Of course there are dangers: of saying too much; of assuming that we know what people need to hear; of not allowing folk to engage with us in conversation about what we say. But there are ways by which we can safeguard ourselves against these things. Anthony Hanson's *The Pioneer Ministry* (SCM, 1961) argued for an understanding of ministry that is always pushing the boundaries, moving out, pioneering. In our witnessing – and that includes, for preachers, in the pulpit – we are engaged in an exploration of the gospel, to see how it might come to expression in someone else's life. We are not there to control either it or them.

Costly it may be, but it is also deeply rewarding. The poem by Leigh Hunt entitled 'Rondeau' could be a cameo of a response to the gospel:

> Jenny kissed me when we met
> Jumping from the chair she sat in;
> Time, you thief, who love to get
> Sweets into your list, put that in:
> Say I'm weary, say I'm sad,
> Say that health and wealth have missed me,
> Say I'm growing old, but add,
> Jenny kissed me.

The poem begins with a surprising first line. Who is Jenny? What age is she? Is this a lover's kiss, or a daughter's, or grand-daughter's? We are only told that her action was spontaneous and welcoming, and the rhythm of the lines adds to the movement of the thought. The poet addresses Time itself, and points out that it will not have the last word about his life; indeed, the ill effects of time which time has brought about on his life are overcome in this one action. Tiredness, sadness, the realization that good health and material prosperity have passed the poet by: all these facts of his life are made irrelevant by that one kiss. The poem ends as it started, leaving our minds imprinted with the sense of Jenny's lips.

Spontaneity takes a lot of preparation. If our witness is to be as valid as Jenny's kiss, then we shall allow ourselves to be shaped by what is going on in our communities, in the lives of the congregations with which we are involved and in the world more broadly, as global issues increasingly affect local communities as well as nations. We need to know, consequently, how to get into the subject matter.

This is a matter of prayer, and thinking, and of the pursuit of holiness. We have to discover for ourselves ways of ensuring that we 'walk the talk', that we live out what we proclaim. There is little point in talking about the kingdom of God in our pulpits and discussion groups and in those contexts where we have a voice in the world, if we do not seriously engage with what this means in terms of our lifestyle and the way we deal with people. Holiness is not the same as wholeness; rather it is a kind of quirk, which verges on the idiosyncratic, and which draws particular attention to the kingdom of God. There are classic texts on the subject, and any library will turn up a list of titles; but we have to carve it out for ourselves.

'Preach the Gospel!', said St Francis to his followers. 'Use words if you must.' Of course we must use words; and we must ensure that those words speak of the new life of the kingdom of God.

———•◆•———

Questions

- When did you last hear good news?
- Where, would you say, does the focus of your faith lie: on the past, the present or the future?
- What steps do you take to ensure that the expression of your faith is contemporary?
- How do you understand the kingdom of God?
- Are you good at talking?

7

Thinking

Reading
Ecclesiasticus 38.24—39.11

The wisdom of the scribe depends on the opportunity of leisure;
only the one who has little business can become wise. How can
one become wise who handles the plough, and who glories in the
shaft of a goad, who drives oxen and is occupied with their work,
and whose talk is about bulls? He sets his heart on ploughing
furrows, and he is careful about fodder for the heifers. So it is with
every artisan and master artisan who labours by night as well as by
day; those who cut the signets of seals, each is diligent in making
a great variety; they set their heart on painting a lifelike image,
and they are careful to finish their work. So it is with the smith,
sitting by the anvil, intent on his ironwork; the breath of the fire
melts his flesh, and he struggles with the heat of the furnace; the
sound of the hammer deafens his ears, and his eyes are on the
pattern of the object. He sets his heart on finishing his handiwork,
and he is careful to complete its decoration. So it is with the potter
sitting at his work and turning the wheel with his feet; he is always
deeply concerned over his products, and he produces them in
quantity. He moulds the clay with his arm and makes it pliable
with his feet; he sets his heart on finishing the glazing, and he
takes care in firing the kiln.

All these rely on their hands, and all are skilful in their own work. Without them no city can be inhabited, and wherever they live, they will not go hungry. Yet they are not sought out for the council of the people, nor do they attain eminence in the public assembly. They do not sit in the judge's seat, nor do they understand the decisions of the courts; they cannot expound discipline or judgement, and they are not found among the rulers. But they maintain the fabric of the world, and their concern is for the exercise of their trade. How different the one who devotes himself to the study of the law of the Most High! He seeks out the wisdom of all the ancients, and is concerned with prophecies; he preserves the sayings of the famous and penetrates the subtleties of parables; he seeks out the hidden meanings of proverbs and is at home with the obscurities of parables. He serves among the great and appears before rulers; he travels in foreign lands and learns what is good and evil in the human lot. He sets his heart on rising early to seek the Lord who made him, and to petition the Most High; he opens his mouth in prayer and asks pardon for his sins.

If the great Lord is willing, he will be filled with the spirit of understanding; he will pour forth words of wisdom of his own and give thanks to the Lord in prayer. The Lord will direct his counsel and knowledge, as he meditates on his mysteries. He will show the wisdom of what he has learned, and will glory in the law of the Lord's covenant. Many will praise his understanding; it will never be blotted out. His memory will not disappear, and his name will live through all generations. Nations will speak of his wisdom, and the congregation will proclaim his praise. If he lives long, he will leave a name greater than a thousand, and if he goes to rest, it is enough for him.

Text

Matthew 24.35

'Heaven and earth will pass away, but my words will not pass away.'

———•◆•———

I was always very bad at handwriting when I was at school; it was, and it remains, illegible. I was punished for it: shouted at, given detentions, told to write things out again, even threatened with being hit for it. But I really don't recall anyone ever telling me how to do it properly. It would be comforting to be able to say that such silly treatment means that I can now command an impeccable calligraphy; but, as you might guess, it did no such thing. My handwriting is still awful, and I still have something of a mental block about starting to write, because I know that it will not be good enough. I don't want to make too much of this; but I do thank God for my word processor.

A scribe is someone who writes, and, when you think about it, Christian people do quite a lot of that. Some people write lots of letters; some write notes of the thoughts that occur to them as they read, especially the Bible; some keep diaries of their spiritual journey; and some write sermons, newsletters, lectures and all manner of other things.

This should not surprise us; to an extent far greater than we think, ours is a religion of writing. It is true, as St Paul said, that 'the letter kills, but the Spirit gives life' (2 Corinthians 3.6); but there is a profound paradox here, if not a straightforward contradiction. For Paul wrote that in the course of a letter, using letters as he did so! And there is more to it than that. For scribes also read; they would have little to write if they did not; and in reading, inevitably, they interpret. And because their writing is informed by their reading, so they have a further interpretative role in what writing they produce for their own readers. So they have to think.

And what a striking image of the scribe we are given in Ecclesiasticus! He is contrasted with the ploughman, the labourer and the smith, all of whom have their place in the scheme of things; but he is devoted to the study of the law of the Most High. Of course the image is patronizing, élitist and sexist, and the rigid social division will not do what is presupposed in it. But the emphasis on working in the context of prayer, seeking out wisdom and exploring the profoundest secrets of life, goes right to the heart of what it is to be a Christian who writes anything at all. It also opens up the fact that the writer must also necessarily be a reader and a thinker.

Many Christian people, even some clergy among them, say, 'O, I'm no great reader', or 'I'm no intellectual', or 'I'm no theologian.' This is not the point. We are not talking Herculean feats of mastery of the complexities of the works of theologians such as Karl Barth or Karl Rahner; the point is to keep the brain active, at whatever level is appropriate, and allow ourselves to be stretched a little. And I know that it is impossible to find the time.

There is no getting away from the fact that ours is a *scriptural* religion, we are one of the 'people of the Book'. So we are committed to reading, and our first text is the Bible. In fact, we don't just read it, we study it. One sometimes hears of postgraduate students in biblical studies being told, 'O, there's little more to be done, now, really!', or of preachers saying, 'I simply do not know what to preach about.' Both of these are nonsense, because texts never exhaust their meaning. Because we are dealing with a real, live text, which always throws up new possibilities for significance and interaction, there are always new things to be discovered, always new readings to be plumbed. Just as science and philosophy and history are always open to new constructions and discoveries, so the text of the Bible provides literally endless paths into the ways of God. Have a read of any introduction to literary criticism – for example, Andrew Bennett and Nicholas Royle, *Literature, Criticism and Theory* (Prentice Hall Europe, Hemel Hempstead, 1999), if you will – and see what fun there is to be had in the variety of ways of approaching any text, including this amazing one which is the Bible.

Writing and reading lead on to thinking – critically. Books are creations, fictions (that's the meaning of the term); and, as Robert Carroll has pointed out, any attempt to say that a particular book is inspired is a covert attempt at controlling how it should be read. But whatever any book says, we find ourselves asking, 'Is it true?' How do we know? What evidence is there?

What is the text up to? One strand of reading in contemporary theory points to the power which the text attempts to exert. This needs questioning too.

Edward Said, in his Reith Lectures for 1993 (published in 1994 as *Representations of the Intellectual*), said:

> At bottom, the intellectual . . . is . . . someone whose whole being is staked on a critical sense, a sense of being unwilling to accept easy formulas, or ready-made clichés, or the smooth, ever-so-accommodating confirmations of what the powerful or conventional have to say, and what they do. Not just passively unwilling, but actively willing to say so in public. (1994: 17)

That, it seems to me, is what the Christian is about who has a passion for the truth of God. Said works this out with reference, as you might expect, to the issue of Palestinian rights, and also to the lack of consistency in American policies of territorial rights and United Nations resolutions. There is something important about truth for the Christian, and it is an issue of public truth. Unfortunately, there has been a tendency in much recent theology to claim that knowledge of God cannot be arrived at by human reason, but only by faith. This has blinded us to the possibility that we might have much to share with our neighbours – not just in the pursuit of justice, which we do up to a point, but also in the analysis of what we can know about the profoundest issues of life, and what factors might be addressed as we work out the ethical dilemmas which present themselves in the complicated world in which we have to work out a living. So we need to develop an awareness that God might be encountered in the processes, the questioning, of things, rather than the certainties – which have a tendency to become idols.

We cannot allow ourselves the self-indulgent luxury of Jesus ben Sirach of thinking ourselves superior to those who work with their hands; and we may not agree that the 'deposit of faith' to which the Pastorals refer has to be guarded at all costs against the predations of the godless in our midst; but we could agree with them on the value of continuing the great scribal tradition, of writing, reading and rewriting the texts of our faith, so that the good news of Jesus Christ is always engaged with the way things are in the world, with an intellectual structure which will enable intelligent and open discussion about its implications.

Many people in our culture are currently finding value in some path of spirituality; it seems that there is a growing need for direction, purpose and some sense of personal identity. These personal searches are taking place at a time when it is becoming difficult to see how, as a society or culture, we might give expression to these human longings, since many of the rewards of affluence are short-lived, and their cost is proving far, far too high in global terms. How might we formulate a way of life and an understanding of it which is contemporary, human, social and forgiving? In the light of what we know to be true about life, how might we go on living and still be happy?

How, then, might we apply our critical thinking capacities to reading and writing the word of Christ? Historical study of the Bible has brought us to the point at which we realize that whatever Jesus of Nazareth said is heavily edited. It has been so developed, expanded, corrected, and so on – and that within the pages of the scriptures themselves – that we cannot hope to identify with certainty what were his very words. The work of the early 'form critics' of the New Testament made that clear, and they identified the role of the early Christian community in generating 'sayings' of Jesus to fit the hour.

So the hope to identify historically, and on the basis of our present texts, any oral tradition that might go back to Jesus can at best be conjecture. We have texts, and whatever underlying traditions there are, unless we have further texts to support them, they remain untestable hypotheses.

So if there is any truth remaining in the saying, 'Heaven and earth will pass away, but my words will not pass away' – and that begs the question as to whether or not any particular saying is authentic – it must be in some metaphorical sense. We have the texts of the New Testament, and we must explore what might be the words – the Word, I suppose! – which God's Christ addresses to us by means of the words which are both attributed to him and said about him.

According to the Letter to the Colossians, Jesus Christ is the 'image of the invisible God, the firstborn of all creation and, indeed, the agent of creation', God's Wisdom, the very embodiment of the agent and epitome of all creation, all that exists.

And just as he is the beginning of creation, so is he also the head, that is the beginning, of the Church. The Church is the new humanity in Christ, understood as a new Adam; and he is that by virtue of his cross and resurrection. And what that brings about is the possibility, the invitation, ultimately for the whole of humankind, and in the meantime for all who will respond to the good news, for forgiveness of their sins, for the possibility of a life made over anew; indeed it implies incorporation, no less, in the life of God by means of baptism into the risen life of Jesus Christ himself.

It is in this context that the Colossians are invited:

> Let the word of Christ dwell in you richly; teach and admonish one another in all wisdom; and with gratitude in your hearts sing psalms, hymns, and spiritual songs to God. And whatever you do, in word or deed, do everything in the name of the Lord Jesus, giving thanks to God the Father through him. (Colossians 3.16)

So the word of Christ will provide the basis for their teaching, moral guidance and wisdom; it will inspire their thanksgiving; and it will provide the motive for every aspect of their living.

That is the foundation narrative: it begins with the creation; it ends with the consummation of all things; and in the middle stands our life together, in peace, in mutual learning and growth, in worship, and in the discovery of Christ in every single aspect of all of those. Our lives will have their endings, even before the big ending; and both they and it may well be apocalyptic. 'Ask not for whom the bell tolls: it tolls for thee.'

Nevertheless in them all, our faith asserts, we shall hear the word of Christ, who in his death and resurrection states that apocalyptic is to do not only with judgement but also with grace: 'Heaven and earth will pass away, but my words will not pass away.'

There is probably a thesis to be written on the principle of 'addition' in Christian theology. We express our belief in Jesus, both as a real man to whom is added divinity, and as the eternal Logos of God to whom is added our humanity; and we approach an altar upon which, by the Spirit and grace of God, to the bread and the wine will be added the real presence of the body and blood of Christ. So in the scriptures, *within* the words, among the many meanings which emerge is also the meaning which is God's word to us; to the human words are added the life-giving, eternal Word of the gospel. These are mysteries, so there is some justification in using the term 'sacramental'.

I write as one who owns, at a rough count of my shelves, 71 individual volumes, in various languages and versions, of a part or the whole of the Bible; and I started to learn it by heart in Sunday School by means of what were called 'responsive exercises'. Each Sunday morning for a quarter of a year, the same passage – a dozen or so verses – was recited responsively. And the same happened, but with a different passage, at afternoon Sunday School. So learning by rote was never a chore; it was a communal activity in worship.

Maybe that is no longer an option for us; but we could set ourselves the task of familiarizing ourselves more with the Bible. Regular reading is the only way, and there are a number of means by which that can be done: arrangement of the books so they are covered within a year or two; notes to assist understanding of a daily portion; and so on. As a student I once put to the test a suggestion made by an American preacher to read the same book of the Bible once a day every day for a month – the same book all the way through. 'Start with Philippians', he said, 'it's quite short, and you can get through it in a short period of time. Set that period aside every day, and do it; and at the end of the month it will be *yours!*' One could say the same of Colossians; it's about the same length. Then move on to something else. There's a thought! But *pick it up and read it! Pick it up and read it!*

But if we want to say that the Bible is the word of Christ, we must note that Christ did not utter it; it is a book written by human authors other than him. Nor is it simply the word of God, without any qualification; for the word of God is the gospel, as 1 Peter 1.25 makes clear: the life-changing word that addresses us as we address the text, whether it is spoken, or read, or explored, or expounded by us and before us.

The implication of this is that the meaning of the Bible is never exhausted, for if the meanings of the Bible are always to be discerned in the process of our interaction with it, then we shall always come to it as people in the process of change and growth, and in different configurations of communities, so its meanings will be endless.

So it cannot be the case that 'what the Bible says' in any one particular text is the last word; for that is always to read it within a particular tradition, with no scope for its being re-read anew in a different context. Rather, the Bible is the first word and the accompanying word, and we have to read it with intelligence, and hear its gospel message as a critique of those dead readings of it and of life which diminish us and our neighbours; the point in reading is to enhance life by the word of Christ, who will always have 'more light and more truth to break forth from his holy word', as Richard Baxter put it.

Bear in mind also that the Bible was written in a language foreign to ours. That adds to its challenge, and to the possibilities of discovering meaning. Neither is it too late to avail yourself of the endless pleasure to be found in learning Greek or Hebrew. A relative of mine found herself wanting to check up on what she had heard in a sermon, so I talked with her about the Greek text, but then suggested that, since she had always been good at languages before studying medicine, she might as well spend some spare time learning to be able to check up the preacher's Greek for herself. She went off and bought a copy of Wenham's *The Elements of New Testament Greek*, and I made her a present of a Greek New Testament. When I last asked, she was doing quite well.

'Do your best to present yourself to God as one approved by him, a worker who has no need to be ashamed, rightly explaining the word of truth.' It is extremely unlikely that 2 Timothy was written by Paul. Rather, it is from the pen of a follower after Paul's death. Wanting to enhance the apostle's memory and reputation, as well as give authority to his own work, he pens these thoughts about the life of the Church and ministry within it. It is fascinating to attempt to get inside the mind of the pseudepigrapher: what is communicated by this text, and what are the subtexts which run through it, given that background?

Clearly, there is a tradition which has to be handed on. Is it the scriptures, the Old Testament as well as Paul's letters, or is it the gospel, or is it what has come, already, to be regarded as 'the right way to do things', or 'what the apostle commanded'? Equally clearly, the text posits the danger of 'false teaching'. So the recipient/s, the putative 'Timothy', must do his (presumably) best to find God's approval, with no need to be ashamed, 'rightly explaining the word of truth', which, presumably, is the gospel; or it could be the texts I have just referred to.

Certainly, for the writer of the Pastoral Epistles, there is a right and a wrong way! The phrase 'rightly explaining' means 'cutting straight'. Maybe it is like slicing cucumber; although, since it is 'workman's work', I suspect that a more appropriate image is that of the judicious slicing of a plank of wood, so that each piece fits where it is intended, as the structure of the good news as it is presented in a manner fitting to those who hear it.

I wonder what priority we give to getting exegesis, or preaching, right? What counts as true, in this field; and what are the criteria by which we would judge? There has to be, for us, some sense that it is in accord with the gospel as it is recoverable in scripture. Paul Avis argued a few years ago that the genius of the Anglican tradition was that it brought a reasonable reading of scripture to bear upon the tradition of the Church, and in that way set a three-way net of criteria for what we might accept as sound doctrine. It sounds very fine to me, but I wonder whether the author of the Pastorals would have agreed? I have a suspicion that he would have wanted a little more 'input' himself.

But the main point is what Alberto Manguel quotes in *A History of Reading* (HarperCollins, 1996: 1): 'Read in order to live' (Gustave Flaubert in a letter to Mademoiselle de Chantepie). Reading sets up the possibility of interaction, creativity, which is the discovery of meaning. Hebrew scribes do it all the time, and add their interpretations to the Law, so that 'it is all Torah', when a tiny passage of biblical text is in the centre of the page, and the Rabbinic exegesis is round the edge of it, with the Targums further out, and so on; it's all Torah!

This is a gospel invitation, to make the most of the Bible – *by reading it*. St Augustine, you will recall, was converted as a result of hearing a child over the garden wall evidently playing a game which involved repeating the words, 'Tolle, lege! Tolle, lege!' 'Pick it up and read it! Pick it up and read it!' And he picked up the New Testament and started to read the Gospel invitation to 'put on the Lord Jesus Christ, and make no provision for the flesh, to gratify its desires'. That invitation echoes down the Christian centuries.

Then, after the Bible, read absolutely anything. Informative, diversionary, subversive, amusing, serious, doctrinal, heretical, anti-Christian, comforting, whatever. Texts are subversive, and meaning is subversive, along with the pursuit of it; and there is no such thing as 'outside the text', for even the so-called concrete realities of the world have to be talked about discursively.

I started reading scientific paperbacks recently – my wife and son explain them to me – having failed to be entered for O-level

Physics. ('Although he has worked well, O-level Physics is clearly beyond his capabilities'.) Peter Atkins on *The Periodic Kingdom* is brilliant, and a glance through the weekly *The New Scientist* is a new world, like Gwyneth Paltrow waking up after being bedded by Joseph Fiennes as Will Shakespeare.

For Christian leaders, of course, reading is a priority far above the meetings and the paperwork from Church House and the diocese. Put time into your diary to do it, and tell people that you have another engagement when there is any attempt to shift you!

I hope most sincerely that you do not find all this simply intimidating. I have become convinced over the past few months that something quite radical must happen to the life of our church and to our understanding of the theological task, if we are to be able to contribute at all to the public good. It will not do simply to mouth the now-forgotten certainties, not of yesterday, but of the day before. By listening seriously to people who want – indeed, some of them say, need – a contemporary framework for handling the religious and spiritual aspects and aspirations of their lives, we could move beyond the obsession with getting them to join us and move out and join them. It might be more fun; but we shall have to apply our critical minds to it! There is an inescapably mental element to faith. And the reality is both that we are all brighter than we think we are and that brain ache can be overcome.

The English critic Frank Kermode has pointed out that we tend to understand our lives on the basis of their narrative. We recall where we started and we note the way we have come; we reckon with death as the end of this present existence; and we shape the middle, our today, in accordance with that. Christian tradition, which has informed that understanding, sets alongside the narrative of our lives a number of other narratives. First there is the narrative of God as we read it in the Old Testament scriptures; then, as part of the narrative of the life of Jesus, there are the many narratives which Jesus himself told: the parables, which draw our attention to the realities of the kingdom of God. Those narratives give way to that of Jesus himself, the stories we have of him, including the over-arching narrative of his place in the plan of God for the salvation which encompasses both us and the whole world. The whole story tells how we owe our existence to God in Jesus Christ; how in him our failings are forgiven and our injuries healed; and who is the goal of our future.

In addition to the narratives are two things: the first is the attempt we make to live out the belief we profess as we respond to the character of Jesus who is the good news which the scriptures disclose. The second is the commentary we make upon it by applying our minds to studying it – and St Paul was the first Christian writer to do that, as far as we know. The regular, reasonable and devoted study of the scriptures is no chore; it is the response to a delightful invitation to explore the depths and heights of the meaning of the gospel of Jesus Christ, who says: 'Heaven and earth will pass away, but my words will not pass away.' The Bible has been the focus of what I have written in this book; and as we apply our minds to the text, it is in its words that we discover the word of Christ, which for us and for our contemporaries is testimony to the good news of the kingdom of God.

——————•◆•——————

Questions

- What do you write, and how much time each day do you spend writing?
- How seriously do you take the 'written' or textual nature of your faith in terms of the time you devote to reading anything at all?
- What do you expect to gain from reading?
- How much time do you devote each day to reading the Bible? What aids do you use in doing so?
- Have you ever thought that parts of the Bible might be wrong? Which parts? How do you bring together such insights into your understanding of your faith?
- In what ways do you think that the Bible, the Church's tradition and reasoning belong together?
- How do you develop your own brain power?

8

Human Being

Reading

Genesis 1.24—2.3

And God said, 'Let the earth bring forth living creatures of every kind: cattle and creeping things and wild animals of the earth of every kind.' And it was so. God made the wild animals of the earth of every kind, and the cattle of every kind, and everything that creeps upon the ground of every kind. And God saw that it was good.

Then God said, 'Let us make humankind in our image, according to our likeness; and let them have dominion over the fish of the sea, and over the birds of the air, and over the cattle, and over all the wild animals of the earth, and over every creeping thing that creeps upon the earth.'

So God created humankind in his image, in the image of God he created them; male and female he created them.

God blessed them, and God said to them, 'Be fruitful and multiply, and fill the earth and subdue it; and have dominion over the fish of the sea and over the birds of the air and over every living thing that moves upon the earth.' God said, 'See, I have given you every plant yielding seed that is upon the face of all the earth, and every tree with seed in its fruit; you shall have them for food. And to every beast of the earth, and to every bird of the air, and to everything that creeps on the earth, everything that has the breath of life, I have given every green plant for food.' And it was so. God saw everything that he had made, and indeed, it was very good. And there was evening and there was morning, the sixth day.

Thus the heavens and the earth were finished, and all their multitude. And on the seventh day God finished the work that he had done, and he rested on the seventh day from all the work that he had done. So God blessed the seventh day and hallowed it, because on it God rested from all the work that he had done in creation.

Text

Ephesians 4.11–13

The gifts he gave were that some would be apostles, some prophets, some evangelists, some pastors and teachers, to equip the saints for the work of ministry, for building up the body of Christ, until all of us come to the unity of the faith and of the knowledge of the Son of God, to maturity, to the measure of the full stature of Christ.

———— • ◆ • ————

How shall we sum up the range of talents which is on offer and which we might develop in order to generate a 'talent for living'? I return to the centrality of living, of being and becoming human. The word 'human' comes from *humus*, earth, so is associated with dust. According to Genesis 2, 'the Lord formed Adam out of the dust of the ground.' So we come back, full circle, to the earth from which we are formed.

Have you ever walked into a dark room and dramatically said either to yourself or to whoever was with you, as you switched on the light, 'Let there be light', and felt, just for a moment, like God?

Jack Miles, in *God, A Biography* (Simon & Schuster, London, 1995), tells the story of the God of the Hebrew Bible, as his character develops from Genesis through 2 Chronicles (the point at which the Hebrew Bible ends). Starting at Genesis 1 he notes that, for all the attention paid in later reflection (pardon the pun!) to the creation of light in Genesis 1.3, the paragraph as it stands in the Hebrew will not bear that emphasis. The words, 'Let there be light' are two tiny words in Hebrew, *y'hi 'or*, and are rather reminiscent of a workman busying himself around his workshop, looking for tools in order to create the work he has set himself. So he mutters 'Light', as he might mutter 'Hammer', or 'Screwdriver'. This is because he has a task to complete, and that is the creation of humankind. The goal of the passage is reached in Genesis 1.26–27:

> Then God said, 'Let us make humankind in our image, according to our likeness; and let them have dominion over the fish of the sea, and over the birds of the air, and over the cattle, and over all the wild animals of the earth, and over every creeping thing that creeps upon the earth.' So God created humankind in his image, in the image of God he created them; male and female he created them.

After that, he takes a well-deserved rest. The whole point of the story is that he wants an image of himself. Light, the heavens, the earth, the sun, moon and stars, the fish and the birds and the animals are *all* precursors to the great creation which is humankind. The same movement of thought can be detected in St Paul's use of this imagery in 2 Corinthians, when he says (2 Corinthians 4.6), 'For it is the God who said, "Let light shine out of darkness," who has shone in our hearts to give the light of the knowledge of the glory of God in the face of Jesus Christ.' There is the same movement here from the creation to light to the possibility of seeing the image of God.

How do the diverse strands of such a variety of created life hang together? What are we here for? What is the world, and what is our place within it? To ask such questions is to acknowledge the necessity of some direction, some purpose, some sense of connection. The Letter to the Ephesians provides part of the answer. Ephesians was written by a disciple of Paul soon after the destruction of Jerusalem in 70 CE. The breaking down of the Temple suggested to the writer the breaking down of the barriers that separated not only humanity from God, but also Gentile from Jew, and therefore humanity from itself. St Paul had preached a gospel which implied the unity of the human race; now this was realized in history, and Ephesians celebrates both the vindication of the apostle and the possibility of human unity in Jesus Christ. That unity is one of diversity, with different gifts, talents and callings; and it is one of harmony and mutuality between marriage partners, parents and children, slaves and their owners – in other words, by implication, for all social relationships. Moreover, the unity of those relationships points to the unity of the whole human race, which is to be found in Christ and which is the destiny of us all.

Belief in the incarnation of God implies the value in the sight of God of all that belongs to the natural createdness of the world. That is why *all* people are called to be disciples, and that is why the fundamental vocation is to 'lay' discipleship, the discipleship of the whole people of God. Baptism is the mark of that, and, even if a person is admitted to other 'orders of ministry' in the church, the calling to be a member of the people of God is fundamental. The Greek word for people is *laos*, and from that we get words like 'lay' and 'laity'. The call to discipleship, to baptism, to Christian life, is a call to ministry; other callings to ministry are dependent upon this one.

This means, not only that there are varieties of ministry in the church which are purely 'secular' – like administrative, secretarial, legal and financial ministries, such as any other institution needs – but also that everything that is created, everything that is human, everything that is fleshy, bodily and material bears the marks of the divine. It means that 'vocation' is not just something which clergy have, but is rather a characteristic of any profession, trade, job or calling in which a person is engaged who acknowledges God as the One who gives meaning to their life.

When the Letter to the Ephesians speaks of 'maturity, . . . the measure of the full stature of Christ', it uses the word for 'man' which has connotations of masculinity. In a way, therefore, it foreshadows the image of the Christian soldier in Ephesians 6. The imagery there is probably more of a corporate, mythical figure, rather of an individual, but the picture of a strong capable, mature human being suggests someone unashamed to be human. John Bunyan's famous hymn, 'Who would true Valour see', comes close to such a picture. The original version retains Bunyan's language, but it has more guts than its contemporary paraphrase; this pilgrim, whether male or female, has a talent for living.

> Who would true Valour see,
> Let him come hither;
> One here will Constant be,
> Come Wind, come Weather.
> There's no Discouragement,
> Shall make him once Relent,
> His first avow'd Intent,
> To be a Pilgrim.

> Who so beset him round,
> With dismal Stories,
> Do but themselves Confound;
> His Strength the more is.
> No Lyon can him fright,
> He'l with a Gyant Fight,
> But he will have a right,
> To be a Pilgrim.

Hobgoblin, nor foul Fiend,
Can daunt his Spirit:
He knows, he at the end,
Shall Life Inherit.
Then Fancies fly away,
He'll fear not what men say,
He'll labour Night and Day,
To be a Pilgrim.

———•◆•———

Questions

- When have you known yourself to be regarded, looked at or looked after and listened to?
- How much time do you devote to developing these talents and using them?
- When have you known yourself to be forgiven, reconciled and growing up?
- What was the last piece of good news that you heard?
- How deeply do you think? What questions are you afraid of asking?
- Imagine yourself as fully human now and describe yourself.
- Will you put some energy into becoming like your description?